Understanding How Asperger Children and Adolescents Think and Learn

Understanding How Asperger Children and Adolescents Think and Learn

Creating Manageable Environments for AS Students

Paula Jacobsen

Jessica Kingsley Publishers
London and Philadelphia

First published in 2005
by Jessica Kingsley Publishers
116 Pentonville Road
London N1 9JB, UK
and
400 Market Street, Suite 400
Philadelphia, PA 19106, USA

www.jkp.com

Library of Congress Cataloging in Publication Data
Jacobsen, Paula.
  Understanding how Asperger children and adolescents think and learn : creating manageable environments for AS students / Paula Jacobsen.
    p. cm.
  Includes bibliographical references and index.
  ISBN-13: 978-1-84310-804-7 (pbk. : alk. paper)
  ISBN-10: 1-84310-804-6 (pbk. : alk. paper) 1. Asperger's syndrome. 2. Asperger's syndrome--Patients--Education. 3. Learning disabled children--Education. I. Title.
RJ506.A9J335 2005
618.92'858832--dc22
                                                                    2005011495
British Library Cataloguing in Publication Data
A CIP catalogue record for this book is available from the British Library

ISBN-13: 978 1 84310 804 7
ISBN-10: 1 84310 804 6

Printed and Bound in Great Britain by
Athenaeum Press, Gateshead, Tyne and Wear

Contents

Acknowledgments

The Asperger children and adolescents in my clinical practice have taught me how they think and learn. Collaborating with these children, their families, and their schools allowed us to work towards providing manageable environments – environments that take into account the way that these students think and learn, as well as how they communicate. This has been a learning process for all of us, and I appreciate all that we have learned, and continue to learn, together.

Julia Hara, a specialized instructional assistant for an Asperger child, kindly allowed me to include her essay, "A Day in the Life of a Specialized IA" (Appendix 1). Pam Ehrlich, the mother of an Asperger child, provided a generic script for a classroom discussion she has led each year in her son's classrooms (Appendix 2). Kathryn Stewart PhD, Director of the Orion Academy, provided an opportunity to observe how a college prep curriculum could be offered in an Asperger-friendly way (Appendix 3).

I decided to write this book when it became clear to me that schools and parents want more specific school and learning applications of the perspective that I first described in my book for psychotherapists (Jacobsen 2003). I was fortunate to have met Kari Dunn Buron and to have her agree to read and comment on my manuscript and allow me to use her Anxiety Curve Model (Chapter 7). Kari has extensive knowledge and experience with Asperger students, and she teaches a graduate level Asperger certification course for special education teachers. Her suggestions were very helpful, and her very enthusiastic response was a wonderful support.

Several other people read my manuscript for me. Nancy Haworth is an experienced fourth grade teacher in the Los Gatos School District. We had never met, and she was not aware of having an Asperger child in her class in the past, but expected to the following year. Nancy provided the perspective of a teacher who was not very familiar with Asperger Syndrome. Jill Hyman had been a special education teacher for school-age children (including those with autism), and has been a nursery school teacher for many years. She brought the perspective of someone who has had special education experience, is interested in understanding Asperger's, has known many children, and is a dear friend as well. I was very happy to have my son, Mark Jacobsen, who teaches English in Thailand, as an enthusiastic and supportive reader. All of my readers made comments and asked questions that helped me, as I struggled to be as clear as I could. My publisher, Jessica Kingsley, raises questions, concerns, and suggestions that help me to articulate more fully what I want to say. It is a pleasure to work with her. And I want to thank my husband Warren, who is consistently supportive of my work and my writing.

Preface

Those with Asperger Syndrome (AS) are often described as having difficulty understanding the perspective of others. Yet understanding them can be as great a challenge for the rest of us. It is not easy to set aside our meanings and understand what something means to someone whose thought processes and references are very different from our own. Some educators may be familiar with AS and recognize the cognitive and social deficits in the children described. This book is an invitation to see who these people with AS are (the way they think), rather than primarily who they are not (their deficits), and to know them as individuals. In addition to understanding the Asperger mind and thinking, this book examines how to support the process of living and learning during the school years in a way that allows the child to know himself, and to experience an educational environment that supports and enhances his strengths and facilitates successes. I use many examples to illustrate the Asperger mind and perspective, the perspective of others, and the problem-solving and communication approach that is informed by this perspective. Examples of specific children are used with permission, and identifying information and situations have been changed. Most vignettes are a compilation of situations that have occurred in similar ways with several children. Books and manuals that describe specific learning and behavior issues, with suggestions for management and accommodations (e.g. Cumine, Leach and Stevenson 1998; Moore 2002; Buron and Curtis 2004) can easily be used along with this book.

Part One

Understanding Asperger Thinking and Communication

Introduction to Considering Asperger Perspectives

Why consider Asperger perspectives?

Even competent children with AS may have difficulty with organization, understanding expectations, homework, and problems working with peers and some adults. As they get older, literature is more abstract, and they are expected to understand what is implied, rather than stated. Creative writing that does not follow a tight structure or learned formula is often an area of difficulty. Deciding what to write, or the act of writing it on paper, can be a challenge.

Behavioral or cognitive-behavioral interventions are sometimes used to modify what is seen as the child's "inappropriate" behavior, to train the child to behave more as typical children behave. Sometimes (perhaps often) this is attempted without understanding the meaning and validity of the child's experience from his perspective. Then, an effort is made to have the child understand what others want, with far less effort made by others to understand him. Educators are concerned that the child needs to learn the skills necessary to navigate the "real world." Some children with AS learn certain things more easily or earlier, others much later or not at all. Trying to accomplish what others want takes an enormous commitment from these children. They are much more likely to want to make this effort when *they* feel it is necessary and when they feel it is possible. This is much more likely to happen when others are interested in knowing them, in making education accessible for them, and not just changing them to fit in.

Learning about Asperger Syndrome

When I began seeing these children, AS was not in the diagnostic manual. They and I could see that they were different than others. These Asperger children and I worked together to understand each other (Jacobsen 2003, 2004). This was a challenge, and it was an advantage. Teachers and parents may have an AS child in their classrooms or in their families before learning about Asperger Syndrome. This can be an opportunity to know a person, rather than a syndrome.

What we know about emotions, the motivation behind behavior, the subtle or "understood" meanings of verbal and nonverbal language, does little to help us to understand these children. They can be "clueless", oblivious to others, oblivious to their own actions and the effect of their actions or statements on others. Their difficulty with empathy may make their comments or behavior seem detached, uncaring, or even intentionally hurtful. Yet they may be very attached to important people in their lives. They often want to do what is right, if they think that they can. At times, they may give up trying to please. It is such a daunting task. These children have strengths, intense interests, and an amazing memory for a great deal of information. Often they are very good at logic and linear reasoning. Their brain seems to process in a very different way.

Teachers need to know what to do

Teachers appreciate specific guides to handling or improving behavior and learning issues in the classroom. They need to manage and teach an entire classroom of students. They may worry that the child will not be ready for the next grade or school, and feel pressured to make this happen. Special education teachers often have fewer students, but the children all have special needs.

The perspective that informs this book is this: be open to learning who the child is and the child's perspective. This is what helps us sustain our attachment to the child. This enables us to have sensible expectations. It enables the child to be open to knowing the world around him, to manage, as best he or she can, in a world of beings that often seem foreign and hard to understand. Try, for the moment, to set aside concerns that this way of thinking and approaching the child will require an unreasonable amount of time. In order to know a child better, a teacher may have to spend more time in reflection, but the teacher may then spend less classroom time trying to manage the child.

Learning Who the Child Is

A diagnosis does not tell us who a person is

Criteria for diagnoses generally identify deficits and what is considered inappropriate behavior in comparison with developmental norms (see DSM criteria for AS, American Psychiatric Association, 1994) – they help us to clarify that something is unusual or amiss. They can tell us *who the child isn't*. A relationship, one with a sense of connection, includes an attempt to understand a person's behaviors from that person's perspective. Behaviors serve a purpose, and are often an attempt at mastery. Remembering this enables us to focus on a person's subjective experience, his efforts to master or to comfort himself. It helps us appreciate and respect the child, because it tells us *who the child is*.

How do we understand others?

It is natural to understand others from the perspective of our own thinking and our own lives, as well as from our training and our theoretical orientation. We generally try to understand those who are different from us in the way that we try to make sense of our own experiences and feelings.

Why do our usual interpretations mislead us with Asperger Syndrome?

It is inaccurate to attribute our own meanings and intentions to the behavior of others, when we do not share many of the same references and thought processes. Many people experience and associate feelings with behavior and language. We see behavior and words as a communication of attitude, interest, and relationship, as well as facts and information. We are aware that we have an emotional effect on others as we communicate. We may assume that others are aware of (or unconsciously intend) their effect on us.

This makes little sense to those with AS. They do have feelings and they do communicate information. What they say and how they say it leads others to assume that they are communicating feelings or intend to affect the feelings of others. They often do not recognize or understand this. They often do not understand what others experience. As one boy I know explained, "I figure out with the thinking part of my brain what other people figure out with the feeling part of their brain." He explained that he used his brain to understand in a very different way than his more typical peers. Some of these differences have been corroborated in brain imaging research studies that demonstrate which part of the brain is activated during tasks that require the recognition of faces (Schultz *et al.* 2000) and emotions (Piggot 2004).

When we have an emotional reaction to the behavior or words of those with AS, our reaction may not accurately reflect the intention or meaning of their behavior. Those with AS live in a world with people who may react in a hurt, angry, or rejecting way. While the person with AS does not really understand this, he can still understand that others think that he is wrong or bad. The person with AS may think that others are wrong, illogical, too sensitive, or even stupid, thus continuing the cycle of misunderstanding, and he may not understand that either!

Why be aware of the Asperger perspective?

It is helpful for those with AS to learn about us. They will not try to do this just because there are more of us, because we are older or in charge. That kind of thinking may not mean much to these children. School can be a more successful experience for the Asperger child and for the teacher of that child, when the teacher has a sense that he knows the child. "Knowing someone" means being open to knowing that person's experience from his or her perspective. With this understanding, learning and behavioral management can be more successful, because they have meaning for the child and for the teacher.

How can wanting to understand help in the moment?

Knowing about the Asperger mind does not necessarily mean understanding a particular child's meanings, behavior, and learning issues at any given time.

Teachers are confronted by the need to handle situations in the moment. Knowing that there is something to understand allows the adult to consider whether there is a real need to respond immediately, such as when safety is a concern (rarely). The adult does not need to take the position that something cannot (or will not) be tolerated, or that something must be done, or must be done a certain way or at a certain time. Remembering that there is something to understand, whether or not it is understood at the time, helps the adult to be kind, even when firm about important issues. Consequences do not have to be punishments. We can be sympathetic when a child is dealing with the consequence of something she did not intend.

Noah

Noah had tantrums and sometimes hit. He was able to stop when others backed off, instead of insisting on something. He was consistently told to use words, if he could, before having a tantrum. Then he did use words at the time of his reaction. He threatened to bring a gun and shoot the teacher and the class. The school had a "zero tolerance" policy for these very words.

Noah was told the policy, and how serious this was to most people. He felt bad afterwards. However, he continued the threats when he was upset. He was sent to the resource specialist when he said these things. She was someone Noah liked, and someone he felt listened to him and understood his perspective. She understood and accepted that Noah was using words, and that there were no guns in his home. She knew he did not intend to carry out his threat. However, she told him, the school had a dilemma, because they had a rule, too. The rule was made because there are people who really do bad things like shoot others, and all threats had to be handled as though they were serious.

Noah did not want to be excluded, although he often did not join in class activities and sometimes left the class himself. He was told that when (not if) he threatened violence, even if he did not mean it, he could not stay in class for that day. The adults at school did not obey the "zero tolerance rule" when they did not take Noah's threats seriously and only sent him to the resource specialist. They were wrong and from now on they would have to send him home when he made these threats. This child was concerned about rules and laws. He continued to present behaviors and reactions that were a challenge, but he very rarely threatened in this way again. Other reactions and statements that might be difficult to tolerate were tolerated for now, and efforts were made to allow him to have alternatives, including withdrawal, when he felt he could not tolerate something.

Classroom management

Children and adults are uncomfortable in a class that is out of control. All feel more comfortable when they sense a teacher's confidence in managing the classroom. Confidence may come from understanding and knowing what to do. Confidence can also come from not being afraid of what you do not know, and an ability to treat a child respectfully even in the face of the anxiety that the child may elicit from the teacher. Classroom management does not mean that every child exhibits self-control and compliance. Teachers who have excellent classroom management skills sometimes have a non-compliant student. Demanding compliance with AS children can result in withdrawal or reactive behavior. Avoiding a confrontation means allowing the student to not join a lesson or activity, to pace, to draw or read a book, to take a time out in a separate area, etc.

Most of us have seen a child become demanding, whiney, tearful, or even have a temper tantrum in a grocery store. When the adult remains calm, even with a flailing child, and leaves the store as soon as is reasonable, others do not generally see that adult's behavior as inappropriate. They see the adult as in control of the situation. The only reaction that most other adults have to this is to be glad that this is someone else's situation to handle that day, not theirs!

Others take their cues from a teacher in the same way. When a teacher accepts behavior that is unusual (or generally unacceptable) from an AS child, this does not invite other students to act in similar ways; others generally attend to the lesson or go on with their work.

A frame of reference

Some find this frame of reference helpful in thinking about the Asperger child's experience and how to help. Although not a true analogy to the Asperger experience with the rest of us, the analogy that seems to help is one in which we might find ourselves in the "alien" role. If we were to spend time in a very different culture, as we tried to learn what is appropriate, we might make faux pas or seem offensive, and we would misunderstand others. We would need to learn new skills, rules, and the meaning of our behavior to others. We would need to find a way to be with others, without trying to become one of them, which we really could not do.

Who would we want to help us, as we struggled to do this? We would need guides who are able to describe that culture in a way that we could understand. It would be more supportive, and less lonely, and it would be much easier to accept help, if our guides were also attempting to understand us, our experiences and frustrations, and adjust expectations to be what we actually can understand and do. It would help if they were interested in our perspective, and respected it as a valid experience. When we realize that the Asperger mind is different, we can work to understand the valid experience of those with AS, as well as focusing on the need for them to develop awareness of the perspective of others.

Al

Al said that he was from another planet. He did not seem distressed or sad as he said this. When he told this to me, he told me in the same manner and tone as he told me his age, his grade in school, his interests, and the names of his siblings and friends. It was information; information that he wished others would understand.

Al became upset or depressed, not because he was different, but because others expected him to change. Al did not notice or understand the nonverbal and implied verbal references in communication. It was difficult for him to answer a question or tell about an experience without going into great detail. His exceptional vocabulary was not adequate for communication. He had difficulty with the more abstract literature and written work at school, as well as with interpersonal communication.

Al understood best what he figured out himself. He could not rely on help, because the explanations others gave him (possibly based on their assumptions about what he already understood or could easily understand) often did not help. He did not know how to ask for the help he needed, and he did not expect the help he got to be useful. Encouragement to "just try," or repeating an explanation, made him frustrated. "Talking him through" an assignment, structuring help with questions that led him to what he needed, enabled him to do that particular assignment. Saying, "See, you could do it," did not match his experience, and was not accurate.

With children like Al, it becomes apparent how much we generally rely on shared understanding and shared ways of thinking and learning. When these fail, it is easy to see the failure as the child's opposition, resistance, or lack of desire. Al knew he did not think like many other people, and often did not understand what they meant. He also understood and could do many things that others could not easily understand or do. Perhaps that is why he thought he might be from another planet. When others began to try to understand his needs, what he did and did not understand, he developed a sense of hope and a desire to understand and communicate with the earthlings around him.

We can understand more. We can accept what we do not understand without feeling overwhelmed or angry. We can avoid alienating the child. All of these are possible if we remember to ask ourselves the following questions:

- What does this mean?
- How does it serve the child?
- How is it an attempt to cope?

What appears to be an unwillingness to do an assignment or participate in a learning activity may have an important reason. If we ask him, the child may tell us "It's too hard," or "I know this already," or "It's too loud." He may say that he needs to chew on his shirt, not stand in line, or to draw and write standing up. When the child answers our questions, it is not useful to see the ways that the child's answer seems wrong to us. It is useful to consider how his answers may be the right answer for him.

A way to look at adult–child relationships

D.W. Winnicott was a child psychoanalyst who was first a pediatrician. He observed and described the relationship between the child, the mother, and the outside world, noting the role of the mother's adaptation to the child's needs (Winnicott 1992). His developmental theories were informed by his observations, and he used the term "good enough mother," a concept that reflected an understanding of the interplay of the child's needs and the parent's ability to respond well enough to meet those needs (Winnicott 1965).

This concept enables us to make sense of the Asperger child's relationship with important adults in his life. The support and interventions that would be excessive for typical children can be the "good enough" support that the Asperger child requires, resulting in more adequate functioning and adaptation than the child could otherwise manage. In school, this requires an awareness of the child, an awareness of what the adults do that is helpful, and a willingness and ability to provide both structure and flexibility. The ongoing nature of these needs is not an indication that the adults have not been effective. The ongoing nature of these needs tells us that the supports and interventions should continue.

3

The Asperger Mind

Understanding cognitive features of the Asperger mind can help us to understand those with AS: what they say, how they behave, and how they learn. The cognitive differences in the Asperger mind explain why some things are easier for people with AS to do or to learn, and why some things are more difficult. Understanding theory of mind, central coherence, and executive functioning can help us understand a child's mind and help us know better what to expect and accept.

What is a theory of mind?

A theory of mind is a concept of another person's mind. If we have a theory of mind, we can recognize that another person's belief is based on his or her experience or knowledge. We can recognize another person's belief even when what that person "knows" is not necessarily what we know to be true. Children with autism often lack a theory of mind. This is sometimes referred to as mind-blindness. Although children with Asperger Syndrome do not have mind-blindness to the same extent, in many circumstances they do not have a very good sense of the mind of another person.

A demonstration of theory of mind

The Sally and Ann situation is a test of theory of mind (Baron-Cohen, Leslie and Frith 1985). Sally is a doll who has a basket. Ann, another doll, has a box. Sally puts a marble in her basket (Scene 1, Figure 3.1, p.22) and then leaves. After Sally leaves, Ann takes the marble out of the basket and puts it in her box (Scene 2, below). Soon Sally comes back to look for her marble. Children are asked where Sally will look for the marble. Autistic children and normal children under four years of age say it is in the box, where they know it is, but which is not where Sally put it before she left. They do not recognize the information that Sally has, and that she can only act on the information that she has.

Scene 1

Sally puts her marble in the basket and then leaves.

Scene 2

Ann moves the marble to the box in Sally's absence.
Observing children judge where Sally will look for her marble when she returns.

Figure 3.1 Illustrations of the Sally and Ann test of theory of mind. From P. Mitchell (1997) Introduction to Theory of Mind, Children, Autism and Apes. *London: Hodder Arnold, p.76. Reproduced by permission of Edward Arnold.*

"Mind-blindness" in autism

Moderate and low functioning autistic people do not have a theory of mind. At best, they can memorize information and rules that may make it look as if they have a concept of mind.

Tom

Tom, a boy with autism, told his mother the outcome of a game without any other information to let her know what he had played in her absence. Tom knew he could not see his mother, when she was gone, but he did not know whether she knew what he was doing. That would require his knowing what could or could not be in her mind. That would require a theory of mind. Tom did learn to say what game he had played, before telling the score. It sounds more appropriate, but does not mean he has any real understanding of why others want that. In addition, the learned behavior sometimes led others, even those who generally knew better, to expect him to understand more than he could.

Tom's mother almost always arrived early and greeted him as he left an activity. One day, she was not there when he got out. He informed an adult that his mother had said that he was to go down the stairs to wait for her. This seemed unlikely, but he was calm, clear, and convincing. He showed the adult exactly where he was to wait, and it was a place that some children did wait for their rides. When his mother came running to get him at his activity, he was not there. She found him, and then pieced together what had happened. Several weeks earlier, when Tom was present, they had another child with them who was to meet them when it was time to leave. Tom's mother told that child to meet her at the outside meeting place. That conversation had nothing to do with Tom or his mother's expectation for him. In addition, that conversation occurred on another day. It was a piece of remembered information. It did not include any sense of why his mother said it, what she might have had in mind, or even the recognition that she had something specific in mind at the time. Tom does not have an awareness of the mind of another person.

How is theory of mind relevant in Asperger Syndrome?

Many children with Asperger Syndrome can understand another person's mind to the extent that they may know what knowledge another person has. They can figure this out, based on whether the other person has seen or heard something. They recognize knowledge based on exposure or lack of exposure to information in the same way they would know what was on an audio or video tape, based on whether the recorder was present and turned on.

One Asperger Syndrome child solved the Sally and Ann test of theory of mind described above. He found it illustrated in a series of drawings, and knew that it was something that people on the autism spectrum had difficulty doing. "I can figure this out," he said when he saw it. He looked at the drawings and the descriptions under them. He thought about them carefully for a while. Then he gave the right answer. This child solved the Sally and Ann situation in the same way that he solves logic problems. He is interested in and good at solving logic problems. He figured out what Sally actually did see and what she did not see.

There is a lot to be learned from this child, because he was able to participate in a conversation that led us both to an awareness of his own discovery of others' minds. He said that when he was younger, he knew that he was real, but he did not think that anyone else was real. I wanted to understand this, because people sometimes say that autistic and even AS children treat them as though they are not real people. He knew others were alive. He just did not know that they were "real," he said, initially unable to explain what he meant. Further discussion revealed that he was aware of his own mind, that there were thoughts, pictures, sounds, and sometimes music in his head. He knew those things were in his thoughts (as opposed to in the outside world). When he was younger, he did not know that anyone else had this experience. This is what made him "real." He realized that others are real when he realized that they had minds, although those minds might be quite different from his and could be hard to understand.

Children with Asperger Syndrome have a theory of mind as it relates to factual information that someone else has. They may learn (perhaps the way that they learn facts) what someone may feel in certain situations, but do not sense the other person's feeling or personal experience as it relates to the information. AS children often have strong feelings and reactions themselves. However, they often do not recognize or understand someone else's emotional experience.

How can we recognize theory of mind issues in Asperger children?

The Asperger theory of mind is often very different from the teachers' or other students' awareness of others' minds. The classroom may be a difficult place for an AS child, and that child may be confusing or upsetting to others who do not understand him. The Asperger child may participate without anticipating or comprehending the response of others. Because we have a tendency to normalize what others say, his participation may be successful. This can even occur when what he meant, and what others understood, were not the same. That tendency to assume that we know what someone intends (based on our own meanings) can work out, but it also can lead to very significant misunderstandings. Others may see the AS child as behaving badly, in an uncaring or intentionally hurtful way.

John

John is a child with strong feelings, yet he does not notice emotional meanings that others understand. This was clearly illustrated in a comment he made in class. John's teacher had been absent for more than a week. When she came back, she told the class she was very sad. Her child had had a serious infection. It resulted in neurological damage that permanently impaired her vision. Someone asked how that could happen, and she shared the medical explanation. John, who is interested in how the human body works, listened attentively. He was visualizing and comprehending the explanation, and then said, "Wow, cool!" Other children and the teacher were shocked.

John did not think it was "cool" that the child lost vision. He thought the explanation of how the body works was "cool." This was hard for the teacher to accept, because the timing of his comment was not sensitive to this sad situation. With an explanation, John understood the teacher's confusion about what he meant. The teacher and the students thought he meant that the loss of vision was "cool." He saw the logic in this miscommunication. The teacher and children were wrong about what he meant, but he did understand what they thought and why. He even accepted that when someone was talking about sad feelings, it was probably not a good time to focus on the facts. That person could then think (wrongly, perhaps) that you just did not care about his or her feelings.

John wanted others to understand what he meant, to understand and agree that the medical explanation was "cool." That is very difficult in a situation like this, difficult for people who want you to focus on their feelings, and not facts, when they are upset. Most people know this, without being told. In this case, accepting his perspective was especially difficult for the others. This is not an extreme example. It is the kind of misunderstanding in social and interpersonal communication that can occur frequently between those with AS and others in their lives.

What is theory of mind in more typical children?

Puppet shows and theater productions for young children may include situations very similar to that in the Sally and Ann test of theory of mind. One character has removed or hidden something, unbeknownst to another character, who returns to look for it. In the test, typical children of four years or older know that Sally will look in the wrong place for the marble, because she did not see that Ann moved it. Young children watching puppet shows or theater productions react emotionally to this kind of situation. They identify what the character knows or does not know, and identify with her. They are upset for her. They feel with a character that does not know where something is, if it has been moved when she was not looking. They sometimes shout out where the object is, to help her. They experience what they imagine is her experience, what they imagine would be their own emotional experience if it were happening to them, along with comprehending the information.

This identification with another's feelings may help a child or adult imagine or understand another person's experiences or feelings. It also may cause a child or adult to assume, incorrectly, that someone with AS intends to communicate feelings, when he is only intending to communicate facts. It may lead to the expectation that the person with AS understands their feelings and intends to be hurtful, or just does not care about them. That is what happened with John and his teacher and classmates. John's classmates were feeling with the teacher and her child, and reacting to the teacher's or their own feelings about what happened. They were not focusing on comprehending information.

Empathy and theory of mind

It is often said that people with Asperger Syndrome do not have empathy. That statement can be disturbing, because many associate lack of empathy with lack of caring or lack of attachment, and sometimes with sociopathic and even criminal activity. At the least lack of empathy is associated with narcissism. Many AS children do care about and can have very strong attachments to people who accept them. Considering that they may not really understand why, it is impressive how much they are willing to do for their parents and for others in their lives. Empathy requires understanding the mind *and* the experience of another person. This is not really possible for those who understand as information what others understand by "feel" and by identification. Empathy also includes: awareness of your effect on others. It includes an awareness of what another person may be feeling as that person communicates with you or reacts to what you are saying.

Asperger children can learn *about* others. These children sometimes study our minds and reactions, and find that cognitive understanding can help them as they cope with us. This is not the same as feeling or identifying with our experiences. They may try to understand, but they often find our ways of thinking very strange and difficult to comprehend. On the other hand, those who are generally empathetic may not be capable of true empathy with those who have AS. Perhaps in that situation, we have to rely on a cognitive under-standing. This does not have to mean we are not attached or do not care.

What is central coherence?

Central coherence is the process of constructing a higher meaning from diverse information. Strong central coherence (global processing) enables one to comprehend and remember the gist of a story or situation. With strong central coherence, one can easily get a sense of the whole and not necessarily focus on the details. In attempting to reconstruct a story, tell about a place, or describe a situation at a later time, the details will not all be remembered. The details that are remembered may not be completely accurate, but the global meaning will be understood and the remembered details will be consistent with the global meaning or gist (Frith 1989; Happé 1997; Lotspeich 2001).

With very poor central coherence (local processing), details are re-membered and focused on without relevance to a global meaning. The details are not considered in relation to a central idea. A lack of strong central coherence has been suggested as an explanation of some of the abilities, even savant abilities, of those with autism (Happé 1997, pp.6–7). Weaker central coherence can explain a strength that relies on an ability to attend to details. Errors in details are less likely to occur for those who focus on and remember details. Finding the problem in a computer program and noticing a detail that leads to new discovery or to new understanding are much easier for those for whom every detail might be important (Silberman 2001; Wheelwright and Baron-Cohen 2001).

How is central coherence relevant to understanding Asperger children?

AS children remember a lot of information. Some refer to them as "little professors" when they share information in an area of interest. They generally do not judge certain facts to be more important than others. Knowing what is relatively more or less important to learn can be difficult or even impossible. They may already know more than the teacher expects them to learn, perhaps even more than the teacher knows, about a specific area. Completing assignments can be overwhelming, if every detail might be as important as another. They may not know where to begin or where to end.

Central coherence has implications for adaptation to environmental changes. With strong central coherence generalizing occurs. Many situations are experienced as similar and therefore familiar. When details are very important, an environmental change may be experienced as very different, something that has to be learned anew, even if most people find the change so small that they do not see it as a change.

Concrete examples illustrate global and local processing

In examining theory of mind we first looked at autism to illustrate the concept. Research dramatically illustrates the concept of central coherence (Bihrle *et al.* 1989) in the processing of visual stimuli by Down's Syndrome and Williams Syndrome children. This research demonstrates that global processing (strong central coherence) and local processing (less central coherence) are unrelated to IQ. Neither reflects greater or less intelligence.

Down's Syndrome and Williams Syndrome are both genetic syndromes that result in mental retardation. The subjects from each syndrome were age and IQ matched. The D of Y's and the arrow of dashes (Figure 3.2) are two of the stimuli they used. In one task, the subjects looked at the stimulus for five seconds, waited five seconds, and then were to draw what they had seen.

The results are dramatic (Figures 3.3 and 3.4).

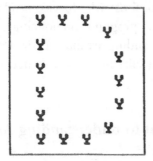 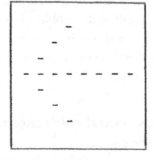

Figure 3.2 Examples of the stimuli. Bihrle et al. (1989), p.42. Copyright © Dr Ursula Bellugi, Laboratory for Cognitive Neuroscience, Salk Institute, La Jolla, CA 9205.

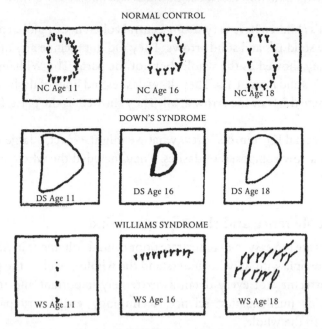

Figure 3.3 Examples of drawings of the D of Y's. Bihrle et al. (1989), p.47. Copyright © Dr Ursula Bellugi, Laboratory for Cognitive Neuroscience, Salk Institute, La Jolla, CA 9205.

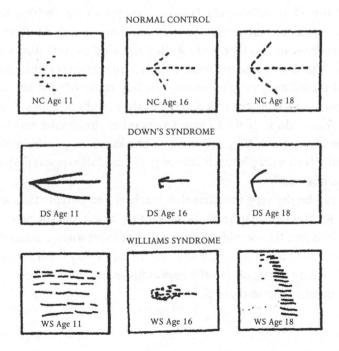

Figure 3.4 Examples of drawings of the arrow of dashes. Bihrle et al. (1989), p.47. Copyright © Dr Ursula Bellugi, Laboratory for Cognitive Neuroscience, Salk Institute, La Jolla, CA 9205.

The Down's children have very strong central coherence or global processing. They drew solid D's and solid arrows. They did not include any of the Y's or dashes. They showed us the whole, but not the parts. The Williams children only drew Y's and lines of Y's. They drew dashes and lines of dashes. They did not recognize the D or the arrow at all. They showed us the parts, but not the whole.

The "normal IQ controls" drew what we might expect, a large D made of Y's and an arrow composed of dashes. They included the whole made up of the details.

Central coherence and the Asperger mind

These tasks are too easy to demonstrate poor central coherence in AS children. However, people with AS who understand the whole as well as the parts often see the correctness of every detail as extremely important and relevant. In certain fields (mathematics, science, technology, etc.) every part can be important to the whole.

Look again at the normal IQ drawings of the D of Y's and the arrow of dashes. These may all be correct to many people, because they represent the parts and the whole adequately. However, they do vary. Perhaps some vary from the original too much to seem correct to someone with AS. If AS children have difficulty with this kind of task, it is the kind of difficulty they might have with school assignments. These children might be very disturbed if they could not reproduce the figure exactly. If they could not picture or did not remember the exact number of Y's in the D, they might get stuck. They might say they "can't" do it, if they cannot remember the details and the whole exactly as they were. If they go on to do the assignment, they may be very unsatisfied, because they know it is wrong. If the adult says it is fine, they may say that is not true.

This can be the very situation that teachers and parents face with these children. A child says that he or she cannot do a task and the adult "knows" that the child can. If the child can be cajoled or otherwise convinced to do it, he may still think it is not right, although the adult may say it is fine. We can see how learning to respond to the expectations of others can be exhausting and very unsatisfying to these children.

Adults can help us understand central coherence in AS

It is common for people to be familiar with details in an area of interest or expertise. However, many can comfortably recognize and describe the global, without the details. Very gifted and competent people with AS often describe the global concepts *and* the details together. They may see both as essential and as inseparable. Global descriptions may seem sloppy to the Asperger mind, glossing over details that they see as an integral part of the whole. A parent with some Asperger traits explained that he does understand the central concept or main idea, and often knows what others think it is. He also pays attention to the details, and said that the whole, without the details, bothers him. In his profession, understanding the central concepts, as well as attention to every detail, is an asset. When helping his son with a project, however, it is as hard for him as it is for his son to do anything less than what he sees as perfectly complete.

The mother of an Asperger child provided a beautiful example of the difference between attending to the central meaning and attending to details as memorable and important. Her husband is a very bright man with a doctorate from a prestigious university. He works in a field in which attention to detail is not only an asset, attention to details as relevant to the whole is essential. Many years ago, he told her a story that he thought she would never be able to forget. She knew she would not remember the story he told her. It had a lot of details with no meaning to hold them together. She clearly remembered the event and its meaning to her, but did not remember the story itself. She was sure her husband still remembered it many years later, and she was right. He told the following story, and said that this story was "a demonstration of a coherent story, in that people will link one detail to the next."

> A glass, half filled with water, is held up against the ceiling by the end of a broomstick. The broom is at a 45-degree angle between the ceiling where the glass is and the adjacent wall, and it is held up by a rose on the wallpaper. There's a string tied around the rose that stretches across the room. The other end of the string is tied around a crystal doorknob. Outside that door, on the street, stands an elephant, with the end of its trunk around the doorknob. The street is strewn with glass ashtrays. Rolling down the street, smashing the ashtrays as it goes, is a Sherman tank piloted by six red army ants.

The friend who told him the story encouraged him to visualize it, rather than memorizing the words, and then repeat it immediately from the pictures in his mind. It was difficult for him to understand why his wife had trouble remembering the story, and thought that perhaps he had neglected to have her visualize it and then repeat it right away. She remembered clearly that he did tell her those things. She did visualize the story as he told it. This helped her repeat it at the time, but she knew that she would not remember it very long. There was no central idea or gist to hold the story together in her memory. Learning about central coherence has given her a cognitive model to help her to understand her son and her husband. It explains the difference between what they remember and think is important and what she remembers and thinks is important.

Central coherence helps us understand school challenges

Ethan

Ethan is an eight-year-old who read easily and answered factual questions to complete school assignments, but generally refused to join the class to listen to the teacher read. When he did listen for a while, he commented or asked questions about the pictures or a character, questions that were tangential or accidentally relevant – he was not following the story. He knew there was something to understand, but not how to figure it out. He recognized this. He was given an opportunity to pre-read books with the language therapist, whom he saw twice a week. She often explained what Ethan could not figure out himself. Ethan welcomed this opportunity, and was then generally able to join the class when the teacher read.

Jim

In Californian schools, fourth grade children study California missions, churches established by Spanish missionaries who travelled north from Mexico to California. A report or project abouth these missions is generally a requirement of the fourth grade curriculum. When Jim had to prepare a California mission report, he was very anxious. He was interested in the missions, and his parents had taken him to visit many of them. He had so much to say, he was worried that he would not be able to complete the report on time.

As the due date approached, Jim expressed more and more anxiety. When the due date arrived, he was not satisfied with his report. He saw it as unfinished, because he knew more than he had written. Jim had to turn his report in the way it was. The teacher would not give him more time. When the teacher returned the report to Jim, his grade was A+. This was a very complete mission report by almost anyone's standards. It did not help Jim to know that the teacher saw this report as complete. In his mind, she was wrong. Most children accept what the teacher expects as the assignment, and they try to do what she wants. Jim did not understand that, and could not accept it when it was explained. He did not agree with what the teacher thought was an adequate report.

Central coherence and theory of mind help us to understand Jim's difficulty with this situation. Jim does not see that the "whole" can be essentially complete to most people without all of the details. It is difficult for him to see that awareness of and understanding what the teacher has in mind is necessary, and as important to school success as understanding factual information.

What is executive functioning?

Executive functioning is the capacity to control our own attentional focus. Executive functioning enables a person to do or to attend to more than one thing at a time. It enables us to recognize what is relevant and shift our attention, to remember or recall what is relevant. Attention, organization, and generalization contribute to executive functioning. With strong executive functioning, we are not distracted by the irrelevant and can shift our focus to the relevant.

Poor executive functioning in Asperger Syndrome

Those with AS often have poor executive functioning. They may not be distractible in the way that others with attentional problems may be. In fact, it may be very hard to get them to shift their attention. The ability to see what is relevant, and shift attention to the relevant, contributes to what is commonly called "attention." It may be difficult for AS children to attend to what others, such as their teachers, see as relevant. The ability to see what is relevant, and shift attention to the relevant, contributes to organization. Those with AS have difficulty with organization, with knowing, remembering, and attending to what is important to others or important in the bigger picture (rather than the details). They also have difficulty noticing the similarity in two or more situations (generalizing)

Determining what is important (most relevant) cannot be taught in a way that AS children can apply. Presenting a situation and a question provides a structure that these children can often respond to. However, it eliminates the "real life" aspect of the problem. Outside of a structured lesson, the child needs to figure out the relevant information *and* the relevant questions. Attention to details, without regard to their relevance to a larger issue (perhaps an issue the child is completely unaware of) makes this an incomprehensible task.

In non-fiction, information is often presented in a direct manner. Some AS children like science fiction or fantasy books. In these books entire worlds are explained in much the way that they would be if they were real. In most literature, a great deal is implied. The reader is invited to understand or wonder about things. This is frustrating to many with AS. It is as frustrating as the communication of most people, the communication that is to be "understood" without being explicitly stated.

Jack

Literature was especially difficult for Jack. He needed information to be factual or logical, and explained clearly and concretely. Once Jack became very angry about a literature book that was a required assignment for his entire class. He tried reading the first page a couple of times. He threw the book down, saying that the book did not make any sense. When asked what did not make sense, he said, "It's the most stupid book written. None of it makes sense." His mother asked him to help her understand or show her the problem. Jack angrily took the book and read the first page out loud. There were references to several people and events that were not explained. In a furious and sarcastic tone, he asked who this or that person was and what this or that referenced event was. His mother asked, "Do you think that those might be the very questions the author wants you to have? Then you can find the answers as you keep reading." His mother's guidance helped Jack go on with his reading, but he still thought that was a very bad way to write.

Jack likes books that give answers and information. He does not like books that have important meanings that are not stated, that invite the reader to have questions without specifically saying what the questions are. Adults with AS, or Asperger-like minds, may remember sitting in required literature classes in high school and college listening to the teacher and students discuss the meanings and the questions that were implied by an author. Several have told me that they believed people were "just making up" what they said, because they did not see any basis for it in the piece they had read.

Those adults with AS whose executive functioning seems, for the most part, adequate have very specific strategies to accomplish this. They may take detailed notes. They can follow the details (pay attention to everything) until they understand the whole. If they are taking notes at a meeting, they may write almost everything and then cross out what they don't need to remember.

This and other strategies may work for them, but using strategies to compensate can be very intense and time-consuming. These strategies are often reserved for specific situations, perhaps for work or situations of great need or great interest. This is generally beyond the capacity of school-aged children.

Central coherence helps us understand poor executive functioning

Strong central coherence (seeing the global, the main idea) is a part of good executive functioning, and weak central coherence (focusing on details without necessarily seeing the main idea, or gist) explains many aspects of poor executive functioning. Attention and organization rely on an awareness of what is important.

Generalizing requires noticing what is most relevant in a situation, then noticing it in another situation. We can generalize if we see two or more situations as essentially similar. Understanding this helps us understand the need for sameness and predictability in AS. It helps us understand why someone might get "stuck" or overwhelmed when something seems very new, rather than similar. Understanding this, along with theory of mind issues, also helps us understand why someone might not notice what others consider important or interesting.

More about executive functioning issues in Asperger children

Asperger children sometimes find it very difficult to attend to an adult when entering a room. They first want to look around, even if the room is familiar, even if it is their classroom. This may look as if they are avoiding the person. They may first need to "check out" the room, to see where things are or, if it is a familiar space, to see that it is the same or to see what has changed.

Jane

Jane is a child who found it very difficult to greet an adult (or respond to the adult's greeting) until she was oriented in the space, even in a space as familiar as her classroom. Her teacher was bothered by this, but genuinely wanted to make Jane feel comfortable in her class. Recognizing aloud that Jane wanted to look around first, asking Jane if she knew why, and allowing this (sometimes commenting, but not criticizing) may have still seemed odd, but it was less odd for the teacher and other children, once they were aware of Jane's need. Jane became much more aware of it too and more likely to respond to the teacher's greeting, even if it was still a somewhat delayed response.

Many Asperger children do not attend to other children. This means that they do not hear what the teacher tells others, often something she intends the class to hear, to respond to, or to learn from. Typical children more often listen when someone is talking about something that could be relevant to them. Sometimes a child is more open to "overhearing" what is said, than when we speak to him directly. Teachers may do this purposefully to be helpful to the children, but Asperger children may not know to attend in those situations. They need to be told directly, in clear and concrete language, especially when what we want them to know is not part of a regular, predictable routine. They need to be told over and over, and calmly, as though it is the most natural thing to be so specific. It is often useless to expect them to notice what may seem obvious to others. As long as the task is understood, as long as it is not too overwhelming, and as long as the child is not exhausted or overwhelmed for another reason, direction and correction that are given in a positive way can be helpful and reassuring.

Theory of mind issues, weak central coherence and poor executive functioning all contribute to difficulties with assignments. Long-term assignments, by their very definition, allow much more time. They also allow for the inclusion of more information. However, poor planning and organization, as well as attention to details without relevance to the larger meaning, and without regard to what others see as important, can be overwhelming to these children. Although teachers break down structural and organizational aspects of these tasks in a way that is helpful and easy to understand for typical children, it may not be sufficient for the Asperger child. Although many teachers make allowances for a child to follow a particular interest, typical children know that it is important to keep the teacher's idea of the assignment in mind. They know that paying attention to what the teacher wants is part of school. They may ask for permission, if they are expanding or changing the focus of the assignment, because they have an awareness of the teacher's mind.

Most children will tell us that school is for learning. Typical children know what is not stated so clearly, that success in school involves finding out what the teacher wants and doing it. Asperger children often do not know this, and when they are told they do not agree. Knowing and remaining focused on what another means or wants is hard. Doing what that person wants, even when they know what it is, may seem very unrelated to what is needed, or may be something they cannot do.

4

Learning the Child's Perspective

We can ask … and then we can listen

It is surprising how much children can tell us directly, if we ask and then listen well. We can assume they have something to tell us, even when their answers do not fit our expectations or beliefs. If we assume they can help us know them, we can try to clarify when they cannot be clear. We can begin by saying, "Let's understand how *you* see this," or "Let's be clear about what *you* mean," before attending to any other perspective. If we then look at another perspective, we can see the conflicting perspectives as a dilemma, something to consider or live with rather than an issue of right or wrong. If nothing else, this clarifies the concept of perspective. Sometimes it takes a while for children to learn how to tell us about themselves. Articulating the things we see and want to understand, in a nonjudgmental way, makes the child aware of what we see. It makes him or her aware of our efforts to understand.

Meaning why when we ask why

When people ask about something informational or scientific, they generally want information that helps them to understand. When people ask "why?" about behavior or communication, they are often *not* really asking to understand. That kind of "why?" is generally used to mean a person dislikes what someone is doing or saying, that they disapprove or disagree. Children learn this very early. They do not ask "why?" when they like what is happening. They ask "why?" when they mean they do not want to do something or do not want to stop doing something or when they cannot have what they want. If we generally ask "why?" when we mean we do not like what they are doing, children are unlikely to think that we are asking to understand. If we are asking to understand, we need to accept their answers, at least as their valid perspective. Even as we observe, if we ask ourselves "why?" in order to understand a child, we are much more likely to accept and feel connected to the child. (See Appendix 1 for an instructional assistant's example of discovering her student's mind.)

Having AS, surrounded by others

Lewis

Lewis is a boy with Asperger Syndrome who knew he was not like others. Lewis brought me a drawing he had made to illustrate this and to help me understand him. It was similar to the picture on the cover of this book, but his original drawing was filled with many blue circles and only one red circle.

"Look at the blue circles," Lewis said. "They are not all the same. Each is a little different from the others. But they are a lot more like each other than like the red circle. The blue circles represent other people. I'm the red circle. That diagonal line through the blue circles represents their line of vision. They are all looking at me and are also looking away from me. Both, kind of, at the same time."

People have said that Lewis's picture and description moved them. This is most likely because, when typical people hear this story and look at his picture, they feel what they imagine it is like to be isolated, different, stared at, or avoided. For Lewis, this drawing was an attempt to communicate information. He did want others to know that they can be difficult for the Asperger child to be with. He did want them to know they can upset him. However, he was illustrating cognitive information about his perspective of the Asperger child in the world. He processes information cognitively. He may understand and care about another's feelings as information, not by feeling them himself. He was trying to create an illustration that would help others to know something about how he felt, not necessarily to feel something themselves. He was pleased to know that others are interested in understanding more about Asperger Syndrome. He had difficulty understanding others, because he did not understand very well how they think and the meaning of their behavior.

Lewis agreed I could use a modified version of his picture for the cover of this book. It has more red circles, representing more Asperger children. They are still in a field with many more blue circles. There are several red circles, and they are different shades of red. The Asperger children are not all the same.

An Asperger perspective on others

AS children are much more likely to try to understand others who want to know and understand them. They do this in an analytical, informational manner. When they do study others, their view of us, their perspective on how we behave, is enlightening. They may find us odd and hard to understand.

Victor

Victor decided to observe and study people he knew who did not have AS. He started with the children in his class, but soon gave up. He saw them as too unpredictable and confusing. Adults seemed somewhat easier to observe. Now and then, he watched what they said or did, and how their faces looked while they were saying or doing something. One day he described observing a teacher and the resource specialist walking across campus, talking to each other. He wanted my help in understanding what he saw. Victor told me that one of the women hit the other one and said, "I hate you!" He watched me as I sat in stunned silence. After a long pause, Victor added, "I know they weren't angry at each other, because they were both laughing."

This was a playful hit, and "I hate you!" may have meant, "you are right!" about something. Imagining a scenario like this helps to make sense of what happened. Explaining this in a way that made sense to Victor was impossible, although I tried. He finally told me not to try anymore. It was too weird for him to understand. He knew that they were somehow playing and getting along just fine, and he had figured that out by himself.

Understanding intention helps us to understand the Asperger perspective

It is easy to attribute intention to another person's behavior. Those with AS are often accused of being purposeful, or of not caring, when their behavior upsets others. The attribution of intention can make those with AS seem bad or wrong. Asperger children (who do not really understand their effect on others, or even when they have an effect) are often told what is appropriate or inappropriate. They are asked to be aware of the meaning of their behavior to others. This amounts to asking them to memorize, remember, and apply rules for behavior that they do not understand. This also means that, to comply and please others, they often try to do many things in what seems like a meaningless way.

Asperger children may sometimes want to listen to how others are affected by them. This occurs when others accept that the AS child did not intend to cause the reaction. When John (in Chapter 3) thought the explanation for his teacher's child's vision disorder was "cool," he did not think it was "cool" that the child lost vision. He was impressed by the medical explanation of what happened to her. He wanted others to understand that as much as others wanted him to know why his comment was upsetting.

Asperger perspectives on school

Many Asperger children say that school is an exhausting place to be; it requires too much effort and attention. Almost everything is too easy or too hard. If they think that they have already mastered the material, they do not need to practice. "It's a waste of time," one child told his teacher about a vocabulary assignment. This may sound rude, but it was information. This boy reads college texts, as long as they are factual, and has no problem understanding the vocabulary. On the other hand, when AS children do not understand a concept or assignment, they may not expect that the explanation or practice will help them to learn.

Well-meaning expectations may create problems

In school, children are expected to be attentive. They are also expected to look attentive. Behavior plans at school are sometimes established to address this very issue. Children are to sit up "properly" in their seats, not fidget, and look at the speaker when listening or answering questions. The intention may be well meant: to increase the child's attention or participation, to have the child look more "appropriate," etc. All of these may in fact bring more stress to the Asperger child, and less ability to participate, because these demands do not necessarily fit the child's way of learning. Sometimes, they distract the child from his way of learning. They may make him more anxious or depressed, more reactive or withdrawn.

Expectations to behave in ways that do not seem natural, or accusations that behaviors (or even the children themselves) are inappropriate, upset and discourage the AS child. Some children can articulate this. "If I concentrate on everything they want me to do," one child said, "I won't have any concentration left to learn anything."

Peer relationships

Often children and parents talk about peer relationship issues and behaviors. As with every other issue, figuring out who the child is and what the child needs is important. Understanding others and how to function in the larger world is then easier to address in a meaningful way. Some Asperger children say that they want more friends. However, if we question them about the other children they know, they may not want many of them for friends. They may just assume that making friends is something they are supposed to do, like reading and math. They do often want to do the right thing, as they understand it. Generally, they do not particularly want to be popular. They want to be accepted as they are. When they are accepted, they are pleased.

The most comfortable relationships that these children have are with those who share their interests and who accept them as they are. They can learn proper host or guest behavior. They can also learn the situations in which they can be themselves. It is important that we recognize and differentiate situations in which they must be conscious of someone's needs or proper behavior. We can help them be conscious of the situations in which they can hang out with someone who does not mind if they leave the room to play a video game, use the computer, or read in the middle of a visit. Understanding their perspective and needs can help us plan meaningfully for them. It helps us to accept and validate their subjective experience and it helps them become aware of themselves and others.

Examining perspective, for the child, is examining his own mind and that of another. Examining perspective allows recognition of one's own mind and that of another. It allows this recognition of mind on an intellectual level. It does not require that one recognize another's mind by identification or empathy. It is much easier to look at another's perspective if ours is understood. In addressing an AS child's behavior, comment, or a difficult situation or interpersonal conflict, begin by clarifying the Asperger child's perspective.

5

Pragmatic Communication
and the Asperger Mind

Pragmatic communication is communication that is understood without being stated. It includes nonverbal communication and implied or inferred verbal communication. Pragmatic language includes recognizing what is relevant to others, information, *and* implications. It assumes shared meanings: meanings that are understood without being stated.[1]

Why understand pragmatic language when working with AS children

Vocabulary, information, and logic are not adequate for "getting" what others understand *without* explanation. The entire school experience, not just the social, may tax a child's understanding of pragmatics. It impacts reading comprehension and creative writing that require understanding the mind of others ("feeling" the experience of others) and shared references. AS children may be baffled and annoyed that teachers ask for information and complete explanations, as the teacher already knows the answers. They do not realize or accept that the teacher determines whether the student understands by having the student explain as though the teacher does not already know. Almost any child will say that children are in school to learn. It is the pragmatic aspect of

---

1   This may depend on an internal aspect of communication (Klin *et al.* 2003) as well as a mirroring ability (Williams *et al.* 2004). Perhaps it is a reciprocal process that the AS child does not recognize, and that is difficult for others to maintain with the AS child.

school communication that helps the typical child understand that school success means finding out what the teacher wants, and then doing it the way the teacher wants it done.

Normalizing communication

Shared meanings are often assumed, even when they do not exist. There is a tendency to "normalize" what we hear. When it does not make sense, we try to make sense of it – to fit what we hear into something that could make sense. Most of us have experienced a conversation in which one person assumes we are still talking about one thing, when the other is referring to something else. We continue for a while, but at some point we know we are no longer in the same conversation. This is cleared up with "I thought you were still referring to…". Both make clear what each was talking about. Both find this funny, because each realizes what he thought (his own mind) and what the other person was thinking (the mind of the other). Awareness of both minds makes it funny.

Typical adults and children may "normalize" verbal exchanges with AS children, assuming that we are in the same conversation, even when we are not. Often this works out. The AS child and the other person may have a different understanding, but it does not matter when both are reasonably satisfied. When a misunderstanding is recognized, we might clear it up. However, the Asperger child may have little or no awareness of how the misunderstanding occurred, and the misunderstanding generally will not seem very funny to the child.

Asperger meanings: Literal and concrete

Many young children love the *Amelia Bedelia* books (Parish 1991). Amelia misunderstands, because she takes everything literally. When her employer, Mrs Rogers, instructed Amelia to dust the furniture, Amelia spread "dusting powder" on the furniture. In another story, she "pitched" a tent by throwing it away. The figurative language is so familiar, and the double meanings so easily understood, that even young school-aged children understand both meanings (both minds) at the same time, and find it funny. AS children may take these meanings seriously, analyzing what Mrs Rogers meant and what Amelia thought Mrs Rogers meant.

Charlie

Charlie, an AS child, asked whether Amelia Bedelia was a child. His question sounded as if he understood her implied, child-like innocence. Charlie was asked why he thought that Amelia Bedelia might be a child. "Look at her face," he said, pointing to a picture of her with children. "Her face is just like their faces." He was responding to a visual detail, not to an awareness of her thinking. Some pages later he said, "She doesn't look like a child here. Her face is longer and thinner."

When children with AS say something that seems to indicate an understanding of subtle or implied meaning, it is best to wonder if there might be a much more concrete way to understand their statements.

Group activities, recess, team activities, and free play

Even very structured group activities rely on understood communication as well as rules. These may seem very unpredictable to those who do not understand. Recess and free play are the least formally structured times. Yet they are fraught with expectations for "appropriate" participation. It is hardly a very restful or "free" experience, when the expectations to understand and participate are beyond the Asperger child's ability. Group activities and team sports that seem very structured to most people may be unpredictable to those who rely on what is stated and do not understand the minds of others.

Can pragmatic language be taught?

Pragmatic language is the social, interpersonal understanding that *cannot* be taught. Assuming that pragmatic language can be taught leads to an unreasonable expectation. It leads to the expectation that those with AS can learn pragmatics, and can then be expected to "get" the unexplained that others just seem to know.

What can be taught?

Most with AS cannot learn pragmatic language, but they can learn *about* pragmatic language. Others can learn the concrete meanings of those with AS and the Asperger child can learn about the meanings of others. This is translating, rather than learning to "get" the meaning. This is raising awareness of self and another, figuring out what has happened between people with different understandings.

Can social skills be learned?

Pragmatic language and social skills lessons that explore specific situations teach rules. Memorized behavior for specific situations does not prepare a child to anticipate and react to a situation that does not fit his memorized script. Lessons that address problem-solving often present a situation or problem. Presented with a problem, the child can learn an expected answer.

In life, knowing the answers to questions and responses to situations is not enough. In life, it is necessary to recognize the questions and the situations. When pragmatic language or social skills groups explore interactions that are happening "live" in the group, they provide opportunities to learn. When the child's perception and that of others are made overt, this provides an opportunity to understand (or see the dilemma). This exposes the child to a problem-solving approach, one that supports awareness and an attempt to clarify. This process can take place in a group, in language or occupational therapy, in the classroom, on the playground, and any other place the child has difficulty, as long as accepting adults are trying to understand the child and facilitate communication in the moment.

Social Stories™ can help

When an adult knows that a situation or interaction is difficult for an Asperger child, a "Social Story" (Gray 2000) may help the child to anticipate and respond to what may occur. Social Stories are descriptions, often with illustrations, that provide a child with information about situations that are difficult or confusing for him or her. They are written from the child's perspective, and also give him or her information on the perspective of others. Social Stories written for a particular child can prepare the child for something specific that adults realize may be problematic. They teach about the things that might be missed, things that may be unexpected or unpredictable.

Can pragmatic language skills and deficits be tested?

In tests of pragmatic language the situations are limited and familiar, the questions are much more clear than in life. True pragmatic language is the practical use of language in life. When a pragmatic language test is given to an Asperger child who has not had social skills or language training, the score often indicates the child's pragmatic language weakness. When a child has had instruction, he becomes familiar with this exercise. Test scores improve because the child knows how to take the test; not because he or she understands the pragmatics of everyday situations. If a child has memorized more scripts, this does *not* mean that his true social understanding has improved. At times, a child may respond with more information than required. If the right answer is there, along with a lot of other information, it is not the right answer.

Jack

A school language therapist discussed Jack's difficulty in responding appropriately to a question. She described a situation to Jack in which he and another boy are walking. He sees that they are approaching a puddle ahead. She asked him what he would say to his friend. Jack gave a long response that included "You'll get wet. Your Mom might be mad. Stop. Don't step in the puddle. You might have to change your clothes." An appropriate answer was included with a lot of additional comments that were not necessary or relevant. Jack did not know what information or how much information to give. He just kept saying whatever came to mind on the subject. He thought about the subject matter, not about the mind of the other person. Although the "right answer" was included, his response was not about knowing the right answer.

Part 2

Addressing and Supporting Life and Learning During the School Years

6

An Introduction to Addressing Specific Issues

How can understanding lead to practical strategies?

When we understand that the Asperger child may be unaware of his own behavior, unaware of others, and unaware of his effect on others, this suggests that the first meaningful step is raising his awareness. Rules and learned strategies about expectations may help the child in a specific situation, but they do not raise the kind of awareness of self and others that leads to understanding and problem solving. We can articulate what is occurring (including more than one perspective, if relevant). We can use very clear and concrete language. This is a practical way to address many situations, a way that can become very familiar to the child and adults.

How can we raise the child's awareness of himself?

We can raise awareness by describing what is "obvious," that is, what may be obvious to many, but perhaps not to the AS child. This means describing the observable, in an informational tone, and in the simplest, most concrete way possible. Describing what is occurring is not correcting it. If we correct something before we describe it, the child may follow our directions without any sense of why we gave them (even when our reasons are clear to us and to most children). An *observable behavior* or situation is anything that could be seen or heard by anyone present. This can be as simple as our noticing the child pacing, humming, chewing his sleeve or paper, standing as he writes or draws, stepping on or moving someone else's project. It may include observing that the child is writing an assignment (or notes from the board, or reading, etc.) and not listening to the teacher talk, or listening to the teacher, but not writing the assignment. That he listens or writes, but not both at the same time, is very important for the child to know about himself (as well as for the teacher to know about him).

How can we raise the child's awareness of others?

Many of these children do not "take in" what others are doing. Directing the child's attention to an adult or another child can also be very concrete and specific. We can say the teacher is giving directions, passing out papers, collecting assignments; or that a specific child is waiting for the computer, putting his paper in the binder, standing in line, using the markers, talking to the teacher. Some children learn to direct their attention to adults, but may be oblivious of other children. If we begin to point out very concretely what we want the child to notice, we may soon be able to ask the child what another child or other children are doing.

How can we address perspective with an AS child?

The most meaningful way for AS children to learn that perspective exists is by having others attempt to understand their perspective. If we keep in mind that people do things for a reason, and try to understand how a behavior or action is an attempt to cope or get comfortable, we are trying to understand the particular AS child's perspective. An *Asperger perspective* is an AS child's possible reason or intent behind the *observable behavior*. The child may be standing to feel more pressure on his hand as he writes or humming to stop hearing other noises. The child's perspective may sometimes make more sense when we consider theory of mind, central coherence, and executive functioning as they apply to *the Asperger mind*. His intent may only be to walk across the room (when he steps on someone's project), to attend to the work he is doing or what he is reading (when not listening to the next instruction). His poor central coherence and weak executive functioning may help us know why he concentrates so well on some things, and misses others. His kind of theory of mind does not include awareness of the experience of another child as he walks through the other child's work area.

How can we help the AS child understand the perspective of others?

When we have articulated *observable behavior* and the child's *Asperger perspective*, when we have attempted to make sense of the child's perspective in light of what we know about *the Asperger mind*, the next step is to consider and articulate the possible perspective of others who observe or communicate with the AS child. *The perspective(s) of others* can also be understood in the light of our understanding of the way that many people typically think and experience the world. *The mind of others* explains the reactions others often have to an AS child. For example, others may believe that the AS child intended to step on another child's papers. For a mind that is aware of others and attentive to what others think, it can be very hard to understand that the AS child can be unaware that he has walked through another child's work area and stepped on that child's papers.

How can articulating awareness and perspective help the child and others to work together?

Learning to recognize one's own observable behavior and one's own perspective is part of awareness of self. With practice, it can support the development of a child's ability to describe and explain his words and actions to others. Learning to recognize the behavior, reactions, and perspective of others is part of learning awareness of the presence of others. After that, it is possible to learn reasons for others' behavior or reactions (as hard as these might be to understand).

When we articulate observable behavior and perspectives, the very different ways of thinking and acting present a dilemma. Articulating *the dilemma* is very different from judging right from wrong, good from bad. Awareness of a dilemma resulting from very different ways of perceiving an experience, communication, or behavior supports kindness and understanding. If something unfortunate, albeit unintended, results from the child's behavior, he is much more likely to correct it (help to fix the project on the floor or wait for another child to finish before talking). Articulating the dilemma may result in a willingness to consider *possible options*, options that may work for the AS child and for others.

In the following chapters, we examine specific situations utilizing the strategy of articulating:

- observable behavior
- Asperger perspective(s)
- the Asperger mind
- the perspective of others
- the mind of others
- the dilemma
- possible options.

7

Behavior

Often an AS child says or does something that seems odd to others. These behaviors occur because they serve the child in some way. Let us examine some of them, utilizing the format described in the last chapter.

Response time

Some Asperger children talk constantly. With some, there is a lapse of time between a comment or question and the response of the AS child or adult.

Observable behavior – difficulty maintaining the pace of responding that people expect, often with no indication that the AS child has heard what was said.

Asperger perspective – unaware of pauses or aware but does not understand why anyone wants a quicker response.

The Asperger mind – often needs to focus first on understanding, then on formulating a response and expressing it. (Everyone needs time to process new information, to formulate the gist while processing the details. This is more difficult for those who do not "get the gist" easily. Even when aware of pausing, AS children must consciously think about saying something such as "let me think" or "just a minute." This conscious attention distracts the responsive thinking and talking that is difficult enough already.)

The perspective of others – people who don't have AS expect a response or acknowledgment that they are heard. They may see lack of a more immediate response as rude, or as anxious or shy. They may feel rejected, annoyed, invisible, or unimportant.

The mind of others – most people who don't have AS are aware of other people's possible feelings and reactions and communicate accordingly, without having to think about it very hard. They may form a hypothesis of the gist without knowing all the details, or may anticipate meaning, and can be formulating a response at the same time as listening.

The dilemma – a child with AS needs to think before he responds, without concentrating on anything else. The other person without AS needs to know that the child is aware of him, that he has been heard and that what he says is under consideration, otherwise he may think the child is ignoring him.

Possible options – the adult could say, "You aren't saying anything," or "I wonder if you heard me?" or "I wonder if you are thinking about (what was said)?" The AS child may consider sharing that he is thinking.

Gil

Gil did not respond to others until he had thought out his response. After several years of working with others who were trying to understand his Asperger experience, Gil started saying, "Umm," when he was aware of thinking and also aware that he was not answering. He did this consciously, and shared his reason. He said that he discovered that this helps others to wait more patiently, while he is "thinking."

Anna

Anna generally remained silent when someone spoke to her. She did not give any indication that she was aware that someone had asked or requested something. Her response, when she did respond, often came after a considerable pause. Anna learned that others who were interested in her and liked her were confused or disturbed by this. Anna began sometimes to say, "I need to think," or "Just a minute." She was proud when this was noted, and explained that she did this on purpose, to help others who were waiting for her response.

Comment

When an AS child does make an effort, it can be to accommodate to the expectations of the outside world, an effort to do what others think is appropriate. Gil and Anna were clear that this way of communicating was not "appropriate" to them; it was not appropriate to the mind and experience of the AS child.

However, even if this effort is only in response to the adult's cueing statement or question (at first), even if it is inconsistent when it comes from the child's awareness (perhaps, after time), it facilitates the relationship, and this is enhanced when a typical adult notices and appreciates this for what it is, something that is done in an effort to do what someone else thinks is important or right.

Eye contact

Many children with AS are noted to have little eye contact or poorly sustained eye contact. Even older children and adults with AS, who have practiced eye contact, often do not use eye contact in quite the same way that most typical people do.

Observable behavior – the AS child gives little or no eye contact; very irregular or brief eye contact; extended eye contact that can seem forced.

Asperger perspectives – people with AS find it hard to look at people's eyes or faces. It can distract from listening or thinking. It requires added, purposeful attention and is only useful to see if the other person is paying attention.

The Asperger mind – focuses on information. People with AS can know (intellectually) that the other person is present and has a mind. They have to specifically think about that fact as separate from the concrete subject or information being discussed.

The perspective of others – people who don't have AS may assume that lack of eye contact indicates lack of attention, avoidance, discomfort, or disrespect.

The mind of others – people without AS may assume that another's behavior means the same as it would mean if they behaved similarly. They use eye contact to regulate social interaction by observing responses to which they attribute meaning regarding the other person's mind. Eye contact and watching faces gives information about the mind (understanding, responses) of another person.

The dilemma – many people with AS do not find eye contact helpful. They may find that eye contact makes talking and responding more difficult. People without AS may find lack of eye contact causes anxiety – it can feel personal.

Possible options – adults without AS can clarify preference for eye contact. They can accept that it does not serve the child the way it serves others. They can accept that it is often not present. The adult can note attention, understanding, etc., in another way (and tell the child what he notices). Perhaps the AS child may glance, or may learn to sustain more eye contact to please others.

Jordon

Jordon said that he has to pay attention to look at someone. He was told, "I don't understand. I thought you can pay attention when you aren't looking at me. Are you saying that you only pay attention when you look at the person speaking?" With that much effort at clarification, he understood the adult's confusion, and could clear this up easily. "I mean, I don't look at people when I talk to them. I must pay special attention to looking, if I look. It takes attention, I have to remember, and then I can't concentrate on listening."

Stephanie

Stephanie rarely made eye contact when she talked to or responded to others. She acknowledged that eye contact was uncomfortable for her. When people directed her to make eye contact, she wanted to get away from them. Stephanie said that she did not want to be disrespectful; she was trying to be comfortable.

Although Stephanie rarely looks at a speaker, she recognizes a request for a response from tone of voice, and can be responsive to the tone. When an adult made a statement with a questioning tone, Stephanie knew that it was a question, and responded. She was pleased that this was noticed. Stephanie also acknowledged that, for her, "looking is always hard, but listening is not always hard." Articulating Stephanie's needs and the expectations of others described the dilemma. As she got older, she used glancing as a tool that satisfies others.

Colin

Colin learned that one reason people look at others when they talk is to see if the other person is paying attention. After that, when he wanted to be sure another person was listening to him, he stared fixedly, unblinking, at the other person's eyes. He seemed able to do that for an inordinate amount of time. This did not effectively regulate communication, and it was disconcerting to the listener. Colin was led to do something that was not natural or meaningful to him. He complied, but the adults got something well beyond what they expected or bargained for!

Comment

A child can recognize that sustained eye contact is not best for him, and learn that eye contact means attention and involvement to others, and lack of eye contact may mean avoidance, anxiety, or even lack of respect. That is not what he means, but that is what others think. He can recognize this problematic situation. He may consider "glancing." Glancing can satisfy the other person.

Many Asperger children can be trained, or train themselves, to have more eye contact. As they get older, they may become more comfortable with this. For most people, eye contact is not taught. It occurs because it is useful. If we remember that, we can notice and be more appreciative of the child's efforts to satisfy others.

Mannerisms and repetitive behaviors

Observable behavior – children with AS may twirl or fidget with objects; flap fingers or hands; pull or twist hair; mouth or chew objects, clothes, or fingers; rock or bounce.

Asperger perspective – these activities are soothing, and may help these children to stay focused. At the very least, these activities help them to stay calmer.

The Asperger mind – these children may be unaware of these activities. They may do these activities without awareness of others, unless others specifically say something. They may (or may not) recognize that others think they are doing a weird or bad thing (which they may hear as information or criticism, but this information is inconsistent with their desire for comfort).

The perspective and mind of others – to people without AS these activities are strange; they look like anxious or distracting behaviors.

The dilemma – the AS child needs to do these things to be more comfortable. Others who don't have AS are distracted and made uncomfortable by these activities.

Possible options – children can meet their needs to engage in these behaviors in more acceptable ways. Other people can understand the need even if the behavior is not socially appropriate.

Aaron

Aaron was a bright, high-functioning eleven-year-old AS child. He was much more rigid than his parents and brothers, liked predictable and structured activities, but was functioning very well with minimal accommodations in a mainstream environment. His only self-stimulating behavior was shaking his hand in his peripheral vision. This was embarrassing, because he knew that others thought it was "weird." This "habit" was something that he wanted to change. He recognized that he wanted others to accept his behavior. The problem was that others were bothered. He did not want to have anyone see him this way, so he tried to stop himself when he was aware enough to do that.

Stephanie

Stephanie, described earlier, pulled her hair out, one hair at a time. She met the criteria for Trichotillomania (American Psychiatric Association 1994). Cognitive-behavioral interventions and medications were not effective. Hair pulling, for this child, was a self-soothing activity. Initially, she was not aware of when she was pulling or whether anyone was watching. So much attention was brought to this behavior that she become more conscious of it.

Stephanie was relieved when adults recognized that hair pulling soothed her. It also left bald spots, and she did not want that. She wanted to have her hair and pull it, too! After living with this dilemma for a while, she had a manicure with long nails, to make pulling more difficult. She remembered that chewing her tongue was soothing and started that again.

Comment

Children who learn to recognize that others are critical of them may wish they could get rid of their self-stimulating habits. They appreciate recognition that these habits help them *and* bother others. This reflects their perspective as well as that of others.

Emotional outbursts: When language fails

Some Asperger children have emotional outbursts. While adults are some-times able to sense what is coming and avoid an emotional "meltdown," this is not always possible. Those who do not understand how overwhelmed the child is at the time may see this as oppositional or noncompliant, and insist on compliance when the child is least able to comply. This increases the child's agitation. At these times, it is impossible to effectively use language to process what is happening.

Understandably, adults often feel the need to address this behavior, and may try behavior plans. The cognitive aspect of a "cognitive–behavioral" intervention relies on awareness. In *The Incredible 5-Point Scale: Assisting Students with Autism Spectrum Disorders in Understanding Social Interactions and Controlling their Emotional Responses* (Buron and Curtis 2004), the authors describe a way to engage the child in recognizing his own emotional state. They suggest a scale of 1 to 5, although this can be adapted to any scale that has meaning to a child. This supports the development of awareness of the child's state. It is not about changing behavior, although that may occur when a child develops awareness. It is not about judgment, either. It is about the adult and the child identifying and labeling the child's experience.

Awareness of the adult's reactions

When Kari Dunn Buron teaches graduate education for teachers, she addresses awareness in the adult as well as the child. The teacher can develop awareness of his or her anxiety. With this awareness, the teacher may more easily know when to respond or not respond.

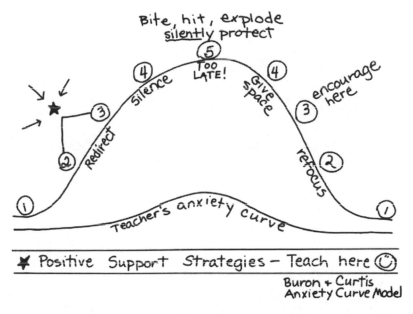

Figure 7.1 Diagram showing Anxiety Curve Model. Copyright © Buron and Curtis (personal communication). Reproduced with permission of the authors.

Once the child and adults have a way to describe the child's emotional state, they can participate in a problem-solving process that includes this awareness, as long as both accept that this process will need to occur when the child is calmer. Using the curve model illustrated here, the teacher's objective would be to help the students to recognize their own "levels" or emotional states. This is simplified by using numbers to label these emotional states. Typically, in level 2 and 3 states redirection is possible. If a teacher can recognize behaviors that communicate a level 2 or 3 state (perhaps by recognizing her own anxiety level) she can be more successful in redirecting or refocusing the student's attention. If the child can learn to recognize his own level 2 or 3 state, he is more apt to "take a break" or otherwise prevent his own loss of control.

8

Academics, Schoolwork, and the Asperger Mind

Children with Asperger Syndrome will often learn when they can rely on adults for support, direction, and understanding; for clarity, structure *and* flexibility; for a patient, non-judgmental, problem-solving approach. Modifying assignments and providing individualized accommodations that reflect the child's needs and abilities makes school less overwhelming and learning more possible. Discussing modifications and accommodations (what they are and why they are used) develops awareness in the teacher and the child. This allows the child to know his own needs and allows him, as he gets older, to explain and to ask for the help or accommodations that facilitate learning, communication, and mastery in his life.

Learning and schoolwork behavior

Observable behaviors – attends to areas of interest, resists other assignments; has a great deal of information, but cannot summarize or get to the point; can be insistent on his view or his way and be argumentative; takes language literally; has difficulty transitioning; forgets or refuses to do work, does not always hand in assignments; cannot decide what to do for an assignment, says he cannot do it, or provides too much detail (sometimes tangential or off topic) in verbal and written work; seems bright and articulate; has difficulty in group work (overly directive or withdrawn); memorizes, or understands information and logic, but does not generalize.

Asperger perspective – school can be an overwhelming place to be, with too much light and noise, and smells. There is too much work and too much to keep track of. Things happen too fast or change too frequently. Work is too hard or too easy. Literature and writing assignments often do not make sense. It is hard to understand or do what the teacher wants. Other children are unpredictable.

Mack

Mack came home from school looking very dejected. "I had to lie today," he said. His mother asked what happened. "We had to write an essay about our favorite thing we did last summer," Mack explained. "I didn't have a favorite thing. I couldn't say that [he would not have known that he shouldn't say that a year earlier], so I wrote about one thing we did. It wasn't my favorite thing, but I said that it was. I lied." Mack's mother said that maybe the teacher wanted them to write about something they enjoyed. "I don't know if she meant that," he said. "That's not what she said."

With this kind of thinking, it is understandable that school can be a stressful and exhausting place to be. Even for a bright child who can handle the academics, the presentation of expectations may not be a good fit for his way of thinking.

The Asperger mind – can focus well on one thing at a time, does not remember to take care of multiple tasks or transition with any sense of being able to get back to something later (poor executive functioning); lacks organization and attention to more than the activity or subject on which it is focusing (this is not a matter of emotional maturity); may be very aware of details; does not necessarily recognize the whole or the main idea (weak central coherence); may have ability to see all the details when understanding the whole (seeing every detail may be overwhelming, but may also be an asset in identifying a missing or incorrect detail in a situation where every detail is important, such as in a computer program). Seeing every detail as important may cause AS children to be overwhelmed and discouraged when they write about something that they know a lot about.

Jim

History was an area of interest to Jim, and he had already read several books about American history when his class studied that subject in fifth grade. He was surprised and upset to find out that they were not going to study the French and Indian War, something he knew quite a bit about. When he asked his teacher about this, she said there was not enough time, and that this was less important than other things that they were learning. Jim did not accept that an historical event was not important enough to study (even for purposes of fifth grade history lessons). He talked to his parents and other adults about this frequently. It upset him so much that he could not let go of it. One person asked whether his teacher would let him tell the class about that war. "Oh, no," he said, "She would never give me the time to do that." When he was asked how much time he would need, Jim said, "Four or five weeks. She'll never let me teach the history class for four or five weeks." And he was right about that.

The perspective and mind of others – others find it hard to fathom how such a bright child can struggle so much when expectations seem clear and straight-forward. It is difficult to understand a mind that thinks and learns very differ-ently; the academic performance of the most capable AS child can be confusing. The child may seem overanxious, sweet, may try hard, be resistant or oppositional, knowledgeable and capable, disorganized, preoccupied or withdrawn, inattentive or overly attentive. Others may worry about the child, think that the child must learn to understand others and comply to expecta-tions to function in the world.

To make the future manageable, first make the present manageable

It is common and very understandable that adults worry that an Asperger child will not be prepared for the future: the next grade, the next school, college, or independent adult life. A stance that the child "must" learn to do what is expected of others is overwhelming to everyone. The most effective way to prepare for the future is to keep the child from being too overwhelmed to function in the present. The best way to help children learn and participate in the present is to ask or require what they can do, and not to ask what they cannot do or what is so hard for them to do at this point that it makes school an unbearable place for them to be. Knowing what a high functioning Asperger child can and cannot do may be difficult, because it is complicated by the appearance, at times, that they are able to understand and do more than they can do, or can consistently sustain.

How can we know what we can expect?

We can observe what the child shows us and listen to what he or she says. These children commonly say they cannot do or learn something, do not understand what the teacher wants, do not understand an explanation or already understand it a different way. They may say that they already know something and it is too easy or a waste of time. We can start by assuming there is sense to their perspective.

It is common for an adult to help an Asperger child who is struggling to "think through" a problem, a concept, or an assignment. The adult may talk the child through it. If the child understands, he can then go on and do this work. When a child follows the thinking of the adult, as happens more frequently with a more typical child, he may be learning the process of thinking something through. This requires that the child can identify (and perhaps identify with) the adult's thought process, and then think in a similar way.

Analyzing and structuring an assignment for an Asperger child may help him to do that assignment. Sometimes an adult may say, "See, you could do it," because it is so hard to see how much the adult's guidance and the adult's thinking contributed. This can happen at times to anyone, even someone very experienced and knowledgeable, helping a child learn. Assuming the child can do what he does not understand is confusing to the child, and it may result in disappointment for the adult.

When a child wants to give up

Examining (with the child) what the child *can* do is the best first step to engaging a child that is giving up. Remember to recognize the enormous effort it takes for these children to remember and comply with expectations that do not seem reasonable or important to them. Unfortunately, it can be much easier to notice when someone is not doing what is expected than when someone is doing what we want. The Asperger child may say and do things that others find odd. These things are easy to notice. It is supportive and effective to notice, articulate, and appreciate the child's efforts, to see what he does do, and together with the child to try to understand why and how he was able to do what he did do. It is less overwhelming when the adult and the child see what the child does well and are patient about things that are not going well at the present time. When a child wants to give up, we can work to engage him in something he can do. Most important, we can try to remember that there is time.

Academic learning and succeeding at school are not the same

Learning information and concepts is not learning to succeed in school. Learning to succeed at school involves understanding how to deal with classroom expectations and work assignments. The teacher and the child will be less overwhelmed if they attend to learning as separate from complying with usual classroom expectations such as completion of work assignments.

Joey

Joey could not keep up with all of his middle school assignments; he often did not know what he was supposed to do. In his class, the students were to look up the words on their weekly vocabulary list, write the definition, and then write sentences that demonstrated an understanding of the vocabulary. While the vocabulary was advanced for many students, Joey knew many of the words already. If he did not know a word, or could not explain it easily, reading about it and talking to someone about it was the best way for him to learn. His test scores were high, but his knowledge was not apparent from his daily classroom and homework assignments, because handwriting was hard for him, and he did not see how making this extra effort made any sense when he already knew the spellings and meanings of the words. If the object was to learn vocabulary, Joey would be best served by taking the test first (orally, if a lot of writing was required), and then only learning the words he did not know well already. If the goal was for Joey to learn to do expected assignments, even when he already knew the material, perhaps one assignment a day would be sufficient. This was a very difficult change for Joey's teachers and school to consider.

Trevor

Trevor has been very interested in science for a long time. In addition to reading and watching educational television and videos, he has participated in "hands on" science enrichment programs at science museums, specialized summer school programs, and science camps. In his high school biology class he was bored with the material and overwhelmed with what he felt was "busy work." Trevor was allowed to take several chapter tests, and he scored from 80 to 90 per cent. As it was recognized that he already had "lab" experience, he was allowed to take a self-paced, teacher-supervised independent study of the textbook. After six weeks of school, Trevor was almost half-way through the book, because much of it was review. Trevor had an Individual Education Plan (IEP) with goals that addressed organizational and pragmatic language issues. The study skills teacher was helping him with organization (other teachers kept her informed when he was missing assignments) and he was given extra time when he needed it. Trevor's school and his IEP team recognized how stressful and exhausting school could be for Trevor, and wanted to support his success in the mainstream. He was trying to keep up on his assignments in many classes, and not making him do that for a subject he knew well already was one way to support him.

Recognizing and addressing learning issues

Other authors have prepared resources for academic educational strategies that are useful with Asperger students (Cumine *et al.* 1998; Moore 2002). When even special strategies are not effective, adults can articulate a child's perspective and try to understand it. If we are prepared to begin with an understanding of a child's view, if we can be patient and very clear about asking the child to consider what he can do, the child may eventually become aware of his desire not only to learn, but to master the academic requirements of a school environment.

Struggles with reading, writing, and math

Some children with Asperger Syndrome have another learning disability in addition to their Asperger thinking and communication issues. Those students may need remediation that addresses the learning disability, and that kind of remediation is more effective and supportive when the Asperger mind and communication are considered. Many children have difficulty with assignments and learning that are related to their AS way of thinking. A problem-solving process with the child may lead to trying something helpful. If it does not work, it is not the child's failure. Adults who understand this can support an ongoing positive relationship that allows both the child and the adult to be stuck for the moment and still have hope for the future.

Reading literature can be very problematic for Asperger children. Typical minds form hypotheses of the meaning as they go along, and adjust them with new information. They do this as they read, whether or not they realize that is what they are doing. For AS children, finding what they already know is hard enough. When they are very young, adults who are reading to them or with them can help them understand. When they are older, reading a synopsis and explanation in advance can help. They can then read looking for the information that they already have. This is not cheating; it is a way to understand. It is very common for people attending operas, Shakespeare or other theater to read a summary of the plot, the characters, and other aspects of the performance, to better understand what they will see and hear. It is in this very way that AS children can read literature. If they know the main ideas first, they can look for evidence of these ideas as they read. They may still think that the implications and impressions that others describe are absurd, but they have a way to get through the material. They can learn that while these impressions are not their perspective, they are the perspective of others.

Some children cannot read on when they are overwhelmed with details and do not understand the main ideas or what the teacher expects them to learn. They may be reading so slowly, in an attempt to understand, that they do not complete this or any other assignment.

Maggie

Maggie was easily overwhelmed with details. She could not continue reading books she had difficulty understanding, even books that were primarily factual. She saw herself, and was seen by others, as a very good reader, and this resistance to completing reading assignments was hard to understand. She could not accept that sometimes it is best to go on, even if you do not fully understand what you are reading. Maggie could not do this. Maggie's school provides books on tape for children who have difficulty reading. It did not occur to most of us to provide this accommodation for a child who reads easily in many circumstances. Books on tape go on by themselves, and for some reason Maggie could tolerate that. She was able to listen to these, sometimes listening two or more times to a tape.

Writing can be problematic for many reasons. It may be the act of writing that is the problem, and for those children, typing may be a good alternative. Learning to type can also be problematic if we want the child to use something other than the "hunt and peck" method, although many people type fast and competently with this method.

Justin

Justin loved to use the computer. By the age of eight his family and school had a strong preference that he learn to type using all his fingers, without looking at the keys. They used a typing program that starts with "home keys." The programs included games to help practice the letters. Justin did not mind playing the games, and memorized the patterns for winning without really associating this with typing words, which he continued to do his old way, resisting attempts to change. Instead of insisting, typing was dropped for a while. Everyone was trying to find something better for him, and hoped he would try again. Later he tried another program, one in which letters are learned in alphabetical order, each with a rhyme (King 1986). Two, then three, four, and then five letter words are learned. He easily learned, and now types everything with all fingers.

For Justin, a teaching method that supported the way he thinks and learns was found. Other children may learn the traditional way. For some children, allowing "hunt and peck" may make better sense than insisting on something that is frustrating and not working. It is this kind of interest and flexibility that supports a positive relationship with a child and keeps him connected to those who are helping, because he will see them as interested in understanding, not just pushing for change.

For many children, knowing what to write can be a challenge. Even assignments with a recommended organizational structure that seems abundantly clear to the teacher and other students may be unclear and overwhelming to the AS child. When the child and the adults are aware of this, they can work to support what the child can write. Sometimes this may satisfy the intent of the assignment, and sometimes it will just keep the child writing something rather than giving up. A child who cannot describe preferences, feelings, wishes, or fantasies may be able to write factual stories. If he is allowed to write facts, then at some point he can be helped to convert them to fiction. He can know that some people use this strategy, and be invited to consider it for the future. It is easier to listen to ideas or thoughts for the future, if they are not presented along with pressure to perform in the moment.

Ben

Writing anything fictional was difficult for Ben. He loved science and liked his seventh grade science teacher. Ben was very upset when his science teacher assigned a paper that was to be a fictional discovery of a known science principle. This teacher was trying to engage a somewhat reluctant class in thinking about the science principles they were studying. The teacher's thinking was something Ben could not understand, although the class was told about it. Ben could not consider that writing what really happened would be acceptable. He was "stuck" and unable to proceed, because he was so sure the fiction aspect of this report was very important, and nothing else would be acceptable. It was only because this was science, which he loved, that he did not want to skip the assignment. On the day before the assignment was due, he finally asked his teacher if he could write nonfiction instead. The teacher was very surprised by the angst Ben suffered and happy to have this motivated science student write about real science principles. Being stuck on one aspect of the instructions, and not on the mind of the teacher, caused a great deal of what could be seen as "unnecessary" anxiety, but this anxiety may be a necessary aspect of living with expectations encountered in the world, from the Asperger perspective.

Some Asperger children seem to be particularly good at understanding math. They may easily solve math problems, but still have difficulty with math assignments. Stephen, described in the next chapter, was overwhelmed when faced with more than four problems on a page. He needed plenty of room to write on his paper.

Maria

For Maria, showing every step of her work was frustrating and seemed unreasonable. Doing many similar problems was annoying, but this was made much worse by the requirement that every step be clearly shown in every problem. Maria's math teacher understood that putting math into language helped understanding, and then communicating what was understood. She wanted to be sure that the children could describe what they were doing. That was the teacher's perspective. Maria's perspective was that she understood the math, and could often get the right answers without writing very much. The teacher felt that although Maria could solve the math problems, being able to articulate the steps was also important. Maria was starting to hate math, which had been her favorite subject, and the teacher did not want to see that. It was reasonable that the teacher needed to know if Maria could articulate the steps. It was agreed that Maria would write all the steps for certain problems (one of each kind) to demonstrate that she could do this. Demonstrating competence made sense. Doing this over and over did not.

Cody

Cody enjoyed math, but dreaded learning a new concept. He could learn during a video demonstration or computer lesson, but did not expect to be able to learn from the teacher's explanation. He became so frustrated and overwhelmed that he reached a state in which he could hardly stay in the room, and could not concentrate on learning anything or even doing something he had already mastered. Sometimes, he left the room. It is easy to see that because Cody had such a difficult history of learning new math concepts with the class, he might be anticipating more difficulty than he would have. Whether that could be true was not relevant; it was not true given Cody's perception. Since he could learn better from the computer or a video, they were used when possible. All concepts were not available that way, and that was a dilemma. It was resolved by inviting Cody (with an instructional aide) to observe lessons in other classrooms without expectation that he would demonstrate anything afterwards. This was a first step in making him more comfortable in the presence of a teacher-led math lesson. It was somewhat like watching a video, but live.

There was a reason why learning to participate in class lessons did not work for this child, whether or not we could figure out what it was. Trying to force what he was not ready for alienated him. Working to understand his needs engaged his cooperation in a problem-solving process, or at least assured him that the adults were considering his perspective and trying to support him.

When the work is too easy, and there is too much of it

Asperger children often complain that work is too easy and there is too much of it. This can be resolved. It is reasonable that a child should be able to demonstrate what he knows. The teacher may be concerned that the child does not understand aspects of an assignment. Doing some of the "too easy" work demonstrates competence. If it is not correct, the child and teacher will know what the child needs to work on. If it is correct, there is no need to practice. Strategies like this support a positive problem-solving relationship that includes mutual understanding and mutual respect.

Taking notes in class

As children get older, the expectation that they will take notes increases. Taking notes means paying attention to what is said and what you think, and knowing what is important to write down. It requires writing as you listen, unless the note-taking environment is specifically adapted to the needs of AS students (as described in Appendix 3). Although the reasons are very different, these children benefit from some of the accommodations that children with reading and writing disabilities receive. They can be given copies of the teacher's notes, they can type, they can copy notes from the board (as long as they are not also supposed to be listening to something else at the same time).

Many successful adults with Asperger thinking take very detailed notes. Some write almost everything or write comprehensive lists. Often they did not develop this ability until late high school, college, or even later.

Learning about succeeding at school

Learning academically is not the same as succeeding at school. If a child is learning well enough (however he learns, perhaps on his own), but not succeeding at school, learning to succeed in school can be a long, slow process. Patience with this process supports the child's chance to develop interest in and the capacity to understand his own needs, and to develop the strategies and communication skills needed to succeed in a school environment. This is much more likely to occur when the child has been understood and supported, and has discovered his own capacity and desire to manage the aspects of school that seem so out of sync with his needs and interests. To help an AS child develop what works for him, allow very small, manageable steps. Knowing and accepting that he can take a long time is much better than giving up.

Learning about succeeding at school

9

The Education Team

Whether or not children with AS have been formally diagnosed, many adults and other children in the school may know and recognize some of their differences. Those with a formal Individual Education Plan (IEP) in a public school have a team that is responsible for planning and monitoring progress. This may include collaboration within the school and with outside professionals who provide other therapies. They are part of a child's support system or intervention team. Private schools, if they are willing, can provide a flexible, supportive team and collaborate within the school, with other professionals, and with parents. With greater understanding, meaningful long-term outcomes (competence, comfort, and independence) may be achieved, especially when the AS child sees this as possible.

In an environment that is working to know the child and facilitate his success, open communication brings a common language to understanding what is observed and experienced. Shared language facilitates everyone's efforts and can clarify how to listen to the child, how to address his comfort and the ways he learns best. Children see the communication between the adults as a support, when they see adults as helpful, interested people who want to know them and are concerned about their comfort. Some children can participate in scheduled team meetings (with preparation). This happens more as they get older, and after they have worked successfully with individual adults. The importance of the positive, accepting, supportive, and respectful problem-solving quality of these relationships is extremely important. This cannot be overemphasized.

Formal and informal collaboration is part of a team approach

Collaboration with parents

Teachers who are interested in understanding AS children can learn a great deal from working collaboratively with parents. Parents often know their child, and know how to communicate with and facilitate for that child. They can share information that enables others to understand and be helpful. Parents may be interested in talking to the child's class about the child and about Asperger Syndrome, particularly in elementary school. This facilitates understanding and a more positive relationship with other children. (See Appendix 2 for a class discussion script.) At times, it is helpful to have a parent work in the classroom to help the child. Sometimes, or with some children, it is best for others to do this. When teachers and parents collaborate to help the child, they make and change these decisions in an ongoing effort to meet the child's needs.

It is most productive to ascertain what *is* supportive and effective about the parent's behavior. When an Asperger child has a parent or parents who interpret and facilitate for him, it can look like over-involvement, like fostering dependence. Often, however, facilitation is necessary and helpful for children with AS. Teachers may also have ways they are successfully facilitating for the child. When the need for support or accommodation is ongoing, this does not mean it is not working. It may mean that the assistance is successful; it is what is needed, and should be continued as long as it is needed.

Collaboration with other professionals

Parents often learn about and obtain services to help their child. Teachers and school teams can benefit from including information from others. The services and interventions from which these children benefit may include occupational therapy, language therapy, group therapy, individual psychotherapy, and specific educational and/or behavioral therapies. Some of these services may be provided at school. Some may be provided privately, in addition to or instead of at school.

Collaboration regarding medications

Some children have psycho-pharmacological interventions. Medications are used to help the child to be more in charge of himself. Managing sensory stimuli can take an enormous effort, especially if the child is trying to minimize self-soothing behaviors that others find odd or offensive. These children often experience anxiety or depression, as they struggle to deal with expectations that do not necessarily match their abilities or their needs. Being at school is exhausting, because they must do consciously and deliberately what most people do with much less conscious effort. With or without medication, it is too much to ask that they do this all the time. Teachers and other school personnel may be asked for specific or general observations when children take medication, information that can be very helpful in planning and adjusting the types and dosages of medications.

Collaboration supports team members

Even very infrequent contact between team members can be an opportunity for support and education that helps the team understand the child and what he can do successfully. On occasion, especially when a child is experiencing difficulty with a particular situation, or with an intervention itself, telephone collaboration or a meeting is needed. Team members can share perceptions of how the situation looks to each person, and how each is responding. Open communication, when the focus is on understanding, supports the child, the teacher (or other adult at school) and the family. To lead to understanding, this must address what is happening from the child's perspective, and the child can and should be aware of this.

Collaboration with the child

Some children can participate in team planning. For children who are convinced that adults believe that they are wrong or bad, having their per-spective and intentions represented is a first step. Talking with the child develops the child's awareness of the issues and shows him the team's effort to understand correctly from his perspective. When it seems difficult and energy consuming for the team to understand how the AS child sees something, it helps to remember how difficult and energy consuming it is for the child to deal with the rest of us.

School observations that support team understanding and planning

Psychotherapists, school psychologists, language and occupational therapists, and educational specialists may observe a child in the classroom and on the playground. They may use observations to determine the need for further assessment, to identify abilities, concerns, impressions, and recommendations.

To be meaningful, observations must be consistent with the teachers' and others' own observations and experience. There should be a sense that all are talking about the same child. In a meaningful school observation:

1. the description should be so clear that anyone present would agree that it had occurred

2. the impressions that follow should be understandable and relevant, as they refer or relate to the observations described

3. the observations and impressions can then lead, also in a very understandable way, to suggestions and recommendations.

Detailed observations enable us to better understand the problematic and successful aspects of the child's school experience, and should note whatever is working effectively. If the team agrees on what is observed, it is much easier to address the implications for a particular child. This leads more naturally to accepting goals and interventions. This is especially true of supports that are needed frequently. It seems to be a human tendency (perhaps all of us do this at times) to decide that if something is working it is no longer needed. Often, if we explore a breakdown in a child's school functioning we find that the supportive interventions were withdrawn. The child was doing better, but only because the interventions, accommodations, and supports were in place. Even if his need for supports continues, as he gets older he can learn to know his needs, advocate for himself, and arrange for the supports that help him.

Facilitating a positive team meeting

The perspective of the person who facilitates a team meeting can greatly influence the effectiveness of the team. If observations and team meetings are focused on a desire to know, to understand and support the child, this position of child advocacy supports the efforts of all team members, including the child. It can help, but it is not sufficient, to know about Asperger Syndrome. That is only useful if communicated clearly and in a way that seems relevant to the specific child. At least one member of the team should be able to state or write recommendations that are clear enough to make sense to the child, as well as to the adults. Often a few clearly stated recommendations for goals and for intervention strategies are enough, but sometimes clearly articulated steps are helpful. The implementation must be relatively easy to accomplish. Recommendations should make it easier, not more complicated, for the child and adults to be successful.

Formal Individual Education Plan team meetings: Preparing in advance

Formal IEP (Individual Education Plan) team meetings can provide opportunities for the team to better understand the child as well as to write annual goals and accommodations. Parents can request reports from the school and share outside reports in advance, which makes for a much more meaningful and productive meeting. It enables team members to give thought to their questions and recommendations for goals and accommodations. The most meaningful and effective goals are based on a true comprehension of what the child understands and does not understand. If benchmarks address the very smallest steps that come next, they address the possible.

Brandon

Brandon was well ahead of other students in his third grade class in reading (decoding and comprehension of facts) and basic math. He also had significant difficulty participating in school, and often read books unrelated to the lesson. When attempts were made to engage him, he became overwhelmed. He cried, pushed, or attempted to withdraw if someone came close to him. Sometimes he ran out of the school, resulting in concerns for his safety. He did not seem to have any capacity to deal with interpersonal issues or problems. In addition, although he liked to listen to books that were read aloud, he was confused and upset when discussion questions were raised, unless they were about concrete facts. Brandon was eligible for an IEP, based on his very poor pragmatic language skills. The following were suggested goals that team members previewed prior to the meeting.

PRELIMINARY SUGGESTED GOALS FOR BRANDON

Social pragmatics goal – Increase awareness and use of strategies to assist with problem-solving.

- Given that a problem has occurred, Brandon will accurately identify the cause of the problem with one prompt 50 per cent of the time.

- Given that Brandon has identified the cause of the problem, he will generate two possible solutions and the consequences of each solution with minimal adult cueing 80 per cent of the time.

Abstract language goal – Increase awareness of and use of abstract language and thought.

- During discussion of a story, Brandon will answer questions such as "What might happen next? What do you think about(…)?" with one prompt 50 per cent of the time.

- Brandon will state whether a question has a correct factual answer or asks for his thoughts or opinions with one cue 50 per cent of the time.

It would be wonderful if Brandon could accomplish these things, but unfortunately, they were far beyond anything he could understand. Brandon did not know why his behavior was a problem for others. He rarely noticed other children, unless they were trying to engage him or interfering with what he was doing. He did not understand the consequences of his behavior or even that there might *be* consequences. He did know when someone thought he was bad and was angry at him, but not why. Also, Brandon did not understand questions that were not factual. To him, "What might [a character in a story] do next?" must be a factual question with a right answer, and he did not know the answer. He did not really understand this question, because it required attention to the mind of others.

The following revisions were made and approved by the team.

Social pragmatics goal – Increase awareness and use of strategies to assist with problem-solving.

- When an adult has identified a problematic situation, Brandon will be able to answer the question, "What has happened here?" descriptively, from his point of view. If he cannot, the adult will describe her observation, in the most specific, concrete language, and ask if he agrees. If he does not agree, she will articulate his view and describe how their views are the same and how they differ (so he can hear both clearly).

- Brandon will listen to the adult's view. If it is different from his view, Brandon will accept (tolerate hearing) that it is a different perspective.

- Brandon will be able to choose from possible solutions that are offered, solutions intended to meet his needs and also to obey classroom and safety rules (e.g., Brandon may need a break. He does not want to stay with the class. The teacher thinks that it is not safe or permitted to go outside, because there is no adult supervision. Brandon can go to a safe corner in the classroom or to another location in the school to rest, read, bounce, etc.).

Abstract language goal – Brandon will differentiate questions of fact and opinion.

- Brandon will identify questions of fact (is it a "who," "what," "where," or "when" question?) as questions about facts.

- Brandon will identify questions of opinion, possibility, or personal preference as questions that do not have a right or wrong answer.

These were goals and benchmarks for the year. The team felt that if Brandon could recognize a situation (as an adult described it) and learn to describe what happened that would be a good beginning. Knowing the difference between questions that have a right or wrong answer and questions that do not have a right or wrong answer would also be a good beginning. If he could do that, he might begin to identify his preference for factual questions and difficulty answering opinion, possibility, or personal preference questions, and eventually communicate that. If Brandon does not respond, the steps are too big and new steps that are closer to his current abilities can be considered. It is this problem-solving process that is important, not a particular solution.

Preparing in advance with a child

With all but very young children, someone can prepare for team meetings or conferences with the child, whether or not the child attends. This may entail as little as making the child aware of the meeting and its purpose in planning to make school a more comfortable place for him to be. It can include exploring issues that concern the child. If someone prepares the child in advance, it enables the child and the adult to clarify the child's perspective and articulate his concerns. It allows the child and adult to examine what has improved or is successful, and what is still difficult or problematic from the perspective of the child and from that of the adults.

A child may prefer not to attend the meeting. It can be difficult trying to listen and understand. Sometimes, especially with an older child, a school requires the child's presence. It should be acceptable for the child to attend a part of the meeting and leave the room as he needs or wants time out from the meeting. This can be stated at the beginning of the meeting with the child and all of the adults present.

Andrew

Andrew was preparing to enter sixth grade. He was a child who had learned to help his therapist, his mother, and his teacher prepare for IEP meetings, which he knew he would start attending next year. He and an adult discussed what would be included, and the adult wrote a list for the meeting. The list was organized into positives and concerns. It included any information that he felt the team should know.

ANDREW'S PREPARATION FOR AN IEP MEETING

1. Positives and improvements:

   a) Does more work in class, cooperates more with what the teacher wants done, concentrates more during lectures and demonstrations.
   b) Still doesn't like how kids act, but this does not bother him as much.
   c) Likes older retired playground volunteer, sometimes plays in supervised team activities during recess. Contact is more okay in this situation (pushing with pressure, as part of a supervised game, is more comfortable than light touching).
   d) Has one friend who lives near him and also goes to the resource specialist's class (can't make more friends because you can't say "hi" to be friendly, you have to say "Hey, dude" and Andrew does not want to do that).

2. Issues, concerns, and things that are hard:

   a) Homework:

      • Forgets or loses homework.

      • Mom may tell him to do the assignment the wrong way (not the way the teacher wants).

      • The teacher said homework could be reduced to half plus one. For an odd number, that would be the larger half plus one. If there are five questions, the larger "half" is three plus one – four. Four out of five is too much.

   b) Math word problems: the assignment is to solve, explain reasoning, and describe a three-step solution for entire assignment. Andrew can find the answer. He can generally explain how he gets it, although that is harder. He cannot find three steps and does not see that there are three steps for all the problems. That may be how the teacher solves the problem; it is not how he does it.

c) Group project: everyone loses five points if anyone forgets or loses work. Everyone is mad at him if he forgets. Answering comprehension questions can make up points, but he sometimes does not know the answers. Other group members should not be punished; he is willing to take his punishment if he forgets or loses something.

d) The teacher said that if there is cheating on tests, the students whose work is copied, as well as those who copy, get a zero. Andrew cannot concentrate if he has to keep looking up to see whether anyone is looking at his paper. (Andrew was asked whether the teacher meant that students should not show their work to someone else on purpose. He was sure she meant more than this. "This teacher means exactly what she says," he explained. Even if he were unaware that someone was copying his work, he was sure he would get a zero.)

The team reviewed Andrew's list. It was an excellent reminder of how Andrew thinks, and why school is so exhausting for him. The teacher addressed issues that were of concern to him, and everyone recognized how disturbed Andrew was by the results of his disorganization. Andrew's IEP had included organizational goals. It was modified to include organizational support. For now, an adult would check his backpack before he left school, to be sure that he had all his assignments and everything he needed to complete them.

Andrew's list helped the team understand how overwhelmed he was by his need to do what he thought was right. His teacher and mother agreed that he would be told to do assignments as his mother understood them. Even if she were wrong, he would get full credit. The "half plus one" modification was changed to read: If there were an odd number of problems, perhaps five, seven, or nine problems or questions on a homework assignment, he could do the larger half and not add one. The objective was for him to know how to do every kind of problem, but that objective was too difficult for him to deal with. He needed a concrete formula.

It was hoped that the organizational support would help Andrew keep up on his group assignments. Andrew's teacher felt that the children were all well aware that there were opportunities to make up points lost by the group, but that was not clear to Andrew. He had enough difficulty participating in a group, even when his role was clearly delineated and he did not have to be part of a larger team effort. He needed to know that the team would not be punished for anything he did wrong.

Andrew's teacher was surprised at the concrete way he responded to her rule about cheating. (It is easy to continue to be surprised by Asperger thinking, even for those who know these children well.) She, of course, did not want him to watch out for other students who were trying to cheat. She wanted him to concentrate on his test.

Andrew's issues with comprehension questions and with breaking down the math problem solutions the way others do were not really addressed. At that point, however, it seemed that the team was becoming much more aware and accepting of the fact that Andrew often has his own way of understanding. His list was very clear evidence of that, and evidence that Andrew cared and tried. Andrew was reasonably satisfied with the changes and clarifications. He felt comfortable that his concerns had been addressed well enough for now, and that people were trying to understand his perspective.

Team planning and formal test results

Test results are often used for determining eligibility and writing goals. Testing may or may not accurately reflect a child's abilities or disabilities. School personnel who assess children with test instruments may not have the skill or the time to interpret the meaning of a particular AS child's test profile. Some children do much better on a test than in a classroom; others do not do well in the test situation, but their reading and math abilities are excellent. They may have difficulty answering if they are not sure of the answer, or if the tester does not tell them immediately whether they are right (which cannot be done in a formal assessment). Others score very well on reading comprehension, because of their ability to remember factual details, but may have difficulty comprehending all but the most concrete material. A neuropsychologist, or a very skilled clinical child psychologist who utilizes some neuropsychological instruments, can often understand and explain the child's mind, and make appropriate recommendations.

Adam

Adam cannot generate ideas for an open-ended topic and has difficulty knowing what to write, because it is difficult to summarize and he does not easily think about or understand what the teacher has in mind. This was not apparent in his school assessment. Adam had worked with an educational therapist, and had learned to write an acceptable three- or four-paragraph essay, using a formula that sometimes worked adequately. In the test situation, one of the stimulus pictures coincidentally was something he understood and had previously written about, and he wrote an excellent short essay. Unfortunately, that rarely happened in real schoolwork and homework situations, situations in which he could spend hours unable to generate ideas, even with help. Fortunately, his education therapist was present, and she helped the team understand what had happened.

Stephen

Although Stephen did poorly on math homework sheets and timed tests, he seemed to know the math facts when asked orally, and could even answer word problems correctly, if presented one at a time. While writing was sometimes difficult, that was not his only problem. He felt overwhelmed when he saw the number of problems on the page. The space for working seemed too small. Understanding the meaning of what the child appears to know, or appears to have difficulty doing, helps establish accommodations based on the child's needs. This child needed to have large papers, with very few problems, well spread out, to do math.

Emotional and behavioral issues

Social–emotional and behavioral issues are often areas of concern. It is in these areas that understanding the meaning of the child's communication, thinking, and particular needs may be most important. AS children generally attend school with students who are different from them. Their social, emotional, and behavioral functioning cannot be accurately assessed by the same measures that are used for typical children. All children are individuals with individual personalities and needs, but typical children are more like each other than like Asperger children, as Lewis's picture on the cover of this book illustrates. Social and emotional goals for AS children may reflect the need for these children to learn how to tolerate or respond to others. We can also understand that the spontaneous behavior of Asperger children may seem odd to others. Others can be helped to understand and accept that.

Social–emotional goals and accommodations

Social–emotional goals are most meaningful if they address a child's understanding of himself and others. In addition, social–emotional accommodations should consider the needs of the child. For example, recess is a time to relax and play, because socializing for most children is a break from structure and a time to have fun. If working on socialization is important, the team can plan structured, supervised opportunities. For these children that is an instructional time, not a break. If a break is important as an opportunity to relax, a school can allow alternatives to playground recess, alternatives that take into account the interests and needs of the child.

George

George is a child who did not like to miss school unless that meant missing the lunch recess. He understood recess as a time he was supposed to play with others. It was noisy. There was too much movement. He walked around the periphery of the playground area, trying to keep away from others, until he could return to the relative calm and predictability of the classroom. If he was supposed to relax after lunch, he needed something else to do, away from all that noise and action.

When George was told that recess should be a break, a rest, he told his mother that he had decided to lie down on one of the benches after lunch. "What will you say if others ask you why you are doing that?" she asked. "I'll just tell them I'm resting," he answered. "They can rest their way. I'm going to rest my way."

The team provided alternative choices instead of playground recess for George. He was very relieved to have his perspective understood and his needs accepted. When he had choices, he sometimes chose to be with others, even though this was work for him. George said that he was interested in having friends. To him that meant he could be around other children who would not be mean to him.

Teams can develop special plans and materials

A behavior plan

Sometimes teams develop specific behavior plans for children, with clearly stated expectations and prearranged cues. The team can ensure that the plan addresses the child's needs and abilities *as well as* the concerns of the school environment.

A reference binder

Particularly in the early grades, a reference binder (Jacobsen 2003, Appendix 5) can support a child who is in a special program, or fully included with or without an aide. A binder may contain information about the child and his current schedule. It may list specific accommodations. A brief summary page can help alert and prepare a substitute teacher or aide. Team members may want to contribute to this.

Informal collaboration between team members

Most contact between team members is informal and occurs on an as-needed basis. This may support a collaborative, problem-solving approach.

Andrew

Andrew, whose IEP preparation was discussed in the previous section, was very disturbed about a long-term assignment he was having difficulty completing. This assignment required understanding of the organization of the material, something that was very difficult for him. He knew he was not able to complete his report on time. Andrew was convinced that the teacher would not accept his report, because when she originally announced the due date, she said there would be no extensions. Andrew could not yet understand that general directions to the class were not always intended for him, even though he knew that this kind of time extension was explicitly described in his IEP, something his teacher agreed to and supported.

Andrew could not consider the possibility that the teacher did not mean him, when she announced that there would not be time extensions. In his mind, she would have said "except if you have an IEP" if she did not mean him. He could not consider the possibility that she assumed he would know that. He was so sure that she did not intend to give him additional time that he did not want to ask. He "knew" that she had been perfectly clear already.

With adult help, Andrew's teacher was consulted about this. She clarified that Andrew would have extra time. She told him that she would not be making special announcements about modifications. He could check with her when she gives general directions that are different from the agreement she has with him and his parents. Even when she says "no exceptions" she may not mean him. It is very hard for Andrew to understand why someone says "no exceptions" when there are exceptions. It is that inaccurate and unclear way in which others speak that he may never really understand. However, adult support facilitates the process of solving these issues as they occur.

Even occasional collaboration can support a cooperative effort

With very high functioning Asperger children, case management may not include specific materials or formal intervention plans. These children may still benefit from the availability of even occasional, less formal, collaboration between the teacher, the parents, and others who know the child. The purpose is always to facilitate understanding, communication, and an opportunity to support the child's strengths while providing the structure and the flexibility to meet his needs at school.

Alternatives to public school can utilize a team approach

Private schools

Most children who attend specialized or non-specialized private or alternative schools do so because parents find a school that is a reasonably good match for their child's needs. The school may be willing to work with the child's needs and appreciate his strengths. Informal or formal collaboration or consultation can still provide observations, opportunities to plan with teachers and other school personnel. These may include team meetings.

Home-school

Sometimes parents decide to home-school a child as an alternative to school placement; others may home-school at an especially difficult time for their child. Outside therapies (language, occupational, individual or group therapy) become part of the home school plan. Wherever the schooling takes place, it is most important to develop a plan that supports the child's education academically, as well as his understanding of himself and others, and supports competence in dealing with other people and life issues.

Special schools or classes for Asperger children

Some public schools have programs for students with AS, with special classes and/or support in the mainstream. These programs can provide a safe haven for AS children who are overwhelmed and affected emotionally by mainstream environments. They have the potential to serve these children very well. The language and social skills curriculum can include acceptance of these children, working with them to understand their own thinking and that of others. There is potential for maintaining a high level academic curriculum, if it is adapted to the AS mind and the AS student's needs, both in the special class and through support and modification in the mainstream.

Private schools identified as schools for children diagnosed with Non-verbal Learning Disorders and Asperger Syndrome have a unique opportunity to provide the education that truly serves the needs of these students in a safe, accepting environment. (See Appendix 3 for an observation report of Orion Academy, a private high school for AS children.)

10

Lessons Learned from and with Asperger Children

In this chapter I describe some Asperger students and the strategies that were developed from the perspective of understanding their strengths and their challenges. There is much to be learned from these children and adolescents.

John

John, a 12-year-old, was genuinely unaware of others. When he talked to someone, he did this without regard to what that person was doing at the time. He was oblivious to what his mother was doing when he talked to her. Many children sometimes do this with their mothers. John did this with everyone. The good news at school was that he paid attention to the teacher. The bad news was that he frequently called out without raising his hand. If he raised his hand, he spoke immediately, without waiting to be called on, as though only he and the teacher were present. He might respond to a reminder to wait, but not remember a few minutes later. Many responses and interventions were tried, some instructive and some more punitive. Nothing seemed to help for more than a very brief time, during which John concentrated on not calling out and was unable to do anything else.

Rather than cue John again and again, the team agreed to focus on directing his awareness to what was happening before he spoke. This seemed important, because John was generally unaware of the mind and even of the behavior of others. John's mother decided to try this. When she was involved in a conversation and John started talking to her, she would say to the other person, "Excuse me one minute, please" (to overtly recognize that person's presence), and then turn to John and asked him to describe what was happening when he came up to her. After he saw that she was talking to someone else, she could tell him when she would be available. If he could wait quietly, he could stay near her. If not, once he was aware that she was busy talking to someone else, he would have to move further from her, and she would come to him as soon as she was finished. This situation occurred often, and John's mother was sure she would have many opportunities to practice it.

A day or so later, John ran up to his mother after school and started asking a question while she was talking with another parent. She gently put her hand out towards John (cuing him to wait), faced the other parent asking to be excused for a moment, and turned to John. She said, "Describe what is happening here." Without missing a beat, John said, "I am trying to talk to you, and you are not listening to me!" It was only after John's mother acknowledged this (his perspective), and asked what was happening as he came up to her, that he finally said that she was talking to another mother. Although he could have been annoyed by this exercise, he knew that it was to help him be aware of what was happening before he talks to someone, to help him know that there is something to be aware of.

In class, John's teachers often had him sit in the front of the room. This made it easier for them to cue him, something he often needed. However, this also supported John's awareness of himself and the teacher, and not the rest of the class. John first needed to develop awareness that he was part of a class. It was best for him to sit where he could see other students. He knew the reason for this, and he and his teacher agreed on a cue for him to note what others were doing.

John may always interrupt more often than most people. For him, the only other choice is to be quiet or withdrawn. The plan for responding to John directs him and others to notice what will give him information, information about when to speak and when to wait, not to discipline him for what seems rude behavior.

Joey

Joey was disorganized, as well as unaware of himself and others. He had difficulty attending to the teacher consistently, organizing or completing assignments, and remembering to follow directions even when he heard them. He concentrated very well when he was working on something, but generally was unaware of other things going on around him. He moved into odd positions, played with any available object, and sometimes made sounds while he was working. All of these things were very apparent from the time he began kindergarten. For the first few years, he managed with very accepting, supportive teachers and a peer who looked out for him, guided and protected him, as much as another caring child can. In kindergarten, Joey was somewhat aware of the teacher, but unaware of the other children, even the friend who noticed him and tried to help him.

As he got older, the class size got bigger and more overwhelming. Joey's parents had him attend a small school with a special education resource class. Although he did not need the resource help, he needed a place to work away from the larger class, and spent most of his day in that classroom.

When he began middle school, Joey had to change class six times a day. His teachers recognized that he was bright, disorganized, and did not stay on task (which meant that he did not switch to the task they wanted him to do), and did not complete assignments (remember to get back to things when he was interrupted). His test grades were excellent, because he knew a great deal of the information already. This child had poor executive functioning. He could concentrate on the work he was doing, but not monitor other things at the same time (even the voice of the teacher or someone calling his name).

Some teachers were concerned about Joey's behavior and attitude. He missed hearing an assignment his English teacher had explained to the class, because he was working on something else. This time Joey recognized that new papers were being handed out, and he went up to ask the teacher what they were supposed to do with them. It was a vocabulary and spelling assignment, and she explained that he was to look up the definitions, write them, and write a sentence using each word. "Well, that's a waste of time," Joey said. It is understandable that this was seen as very rude, from the teacher's perspective. From Joey's perspective, this was a statement of fact. This assignment was a waste of time for him. He knew the spelling and definitions. He could use these words correctly already, and often did. However, by ordinary grading standards Joey would fail almost all his classes. This school did not yet know how to adjust requirements adequately to support Joey. He was not mastering the social and interpersonal aspects of basic survival at school, and was assigned an aide with a focus on controlling and modifying his behaviors. Joey did not see how this could help. "If I pay attention to everything she wants me to," he said, "I won't have any attention left to do anything else."

A class for higher functioning Asperger students would have been ideal for Joey, but did not exist in his community. After a year of middle school, Joey was home-schooled, with a plan to reintegrate him into a school later. At home, he learned strategies for writing paragraphs and essays. He had outings in which he studied other people, first with a language therapist. Joey studied people as a scientist would study a foreign organism. He learned, in an intellectual way, a lot about typical humans and how they act. He considered how to relate to them, and even thought back to his earlier experiences. Joey says the friend who helped him in grade school knew him since kindergarten, but he only knew his friend since first grade. He recognized that he was completely unaware of other children in kindergarten, even the child who helped him. "I didn't know who any of the other children were when I was in kindergarten," Joey said. After thinking about this a moment, he added, "But I think that all of the other children knew who I was!"

Joey is preparing himself to attend eleventh and twelfth grade at an alternative public high school on a community college campus. He calls his very conscious way of being with others, without standing out as too different, being like a chameleon. It can be exhausting, because it takes a lot of effort. At least some of the time this has been successful, although not completely. "But then," Joey says, "even a chameleon isn't invisible."

Dan

Dan was a ten-year-old who developed an interest in people's minds. As he worked on this, he paid more attention in interpersonal situations and even to the teachers at school. Homework, however, was an ongoing challenge, as was keeping track of his assignments. He was exhausted after spending most of the day in school. He needed time to rest in his room, to engage in a repetitive stereotypical movement that helped him to relax. Although he wanted help from adults, he had difficulty accepting modifications that would mean doing less work.

By agreement with the school, Dan's parents could shorten his assignments, and he knew this. They did this by keeping what seemed to be most relevant. To Dan, it seemed that shortening assignments was based on an arbitrary guess and not likely to prepare him for tests. He could not comprehend that his parents could accurately discern the most important information or what was most relevant. Only knowing everything would do that, and there was not enough time to learn everything. Time was more important, because Dan was an excruciatingly slow reader, although he could read words and sentences quickly. Dan figured out why, with adults who were trying to understand his perspective. He read slowly, because every word might be important to understand.

Understanding central coherence helped Dan, along with learning to consciously attend to others' minds (such as the teacher's mind and her perspective on an assignment). He learned that there were central concepts that were more obvious to some people. Dan worried that his parent's idea of the main idea, of what might be important, might not be the same as his teacher's. He thought that his parent might be wrong about what his teacher would see as most important. He did understand that he needed to stop working after a fixed amount of time. This made sense to him, because it was very apparent that he did not work fast enough to finish. His teacher, his parents, and he agreed that after working on an assignment for 45 minutes he was to stop.

The next year, Dan's social studies teacher was giving students an opportunity to develop tools that might help them as they learned new material. She asked the students to skim the chapter before reading it. They were to do this in a relatively short time. She wanted to give them the sense that they could understand main ideas quickly, and then learn more about the particulars later. This way of learning was useless to Dan. He was very disturbed by what he understood to be a requirement. He now thought that reading slowly and remembering every detail was wrong. It was not really doing the assignment. It might even be a kind of cheating. This became one of the topics Dan raised for discussion at a team meeting. It was an opportunity to understand Dan's perspective and his teacher's perspective. This teacher only wanted him to skim, if that could be a useful tool for him to learn. This had to be clarified in order for him to be reassured that he was not failing to do his work the right way. Then he could move on.

Dan started to understand that there was a main idea that many others understood quickly. He could not conceive of understanding the main idea without all the details, and sometimes did not understand it even when he knew all the details. He began to ask people he trusted to tell him how some people knew the main idea. He wanted to learn how. Of course, that is something that cannot be explained, any more than he could instruct others on how to attend to and remember so many details, something he often does easily.

Josh

In kindergarten Josh spent a considerable amount of time under the table. In later grades, he often read by himself, whenever possible. He was interested in and mastered subjects that required memory of facts and logical thinking.

Although he sometimes forgot to do or to turn in assignments, he became a good math, science, and history student. His test scores in these subjects were generally excellent. Spelling and vocabulary were easy for him, and he enjoyed formulaic fiction. Other literature and creative writing assignments were hard for him, because he did not really understand what others wanted. He did not even understand when others tried to explain or help him.

For many years Josh did not tell anyone that he needed help. He did not want to try to write something that did not make sense to him. Although many attempts were made to help him, by teachers and his parents, he experienced these as unreasonable pressure, something that made him more anxious and less able to do any of his work. Josh was invited to consider help in the future, when he was ready. Suggestions that he might want to consider were occasionally mentioned. These included writing something that was true, and then changing it to fit a fiction assignment, or letting someone help him by explaining or outlining possibilities. He was resistant to listening to this for more than the briefest time, and he was not open to considering these suggestions for a long time.

As Josh became older, he started to care about his grades, and as he prepared to start high school, he expressed the determination to learn to work around these issues. He knew that he did not understand people very well, which made certain kinds of literature and writing assignments very difficult. He began by allowing his mother to organize and talk him through an assignment, on occasion, in middle school. He then filled in the details. Once in high school, he started explaining his difficulty to his teachers. He accepted help, a formula or a modification in the assignment.

Josh knew that he had difficulty keeping track of his assignments. He could easily forget to do something or to turn it in if he did it. He was very worried about this, and decided that the organization suggested by one teacher worked best for him. He filed his papers into three sections of his binder. He put all work that had to be done in the first section. In the second section, he put all completed work that he needed to turn in. When work was returned to him, he put it in the third section. When Josh's determination for mastery was noticed, he responded very matter-of-factly, "I have to do it. I'm in high school now. Everything I do goes on my permanent record."

Heidi

Heidi, a bright, high functioning ten-year-old, did not have friends outside her family. She said that she wanted the other girls to like her, but at the same time found it hard to tolerate them. Heidi is a child who likes expectations to be clear and predictable. Although she prefers clear expectations and structure, consistently meeting these exhausts her. She chooses to do very few outside activities.

Certain school assignments are particularly difficult for Heidi. She may not know how to write the essay, speech, or poem that has been assigned. However, unlike many AS children who then get "stuck," she writes what she can write, and is willing to accept help adapting what she wrote to the assignment, when that makes sense to her. This has become her strategy for handling the kinds of assignments that are often difficult for the most academically successful Asperger children.

Once Heidi had to write a speech to celebrate a major anniversary of her school. She did what she often does in this kind of assignment. She used an example as a model; in this case she used the Gettysburg Address. With some help with vocabulary, she wrote a speech beginning in the format: "Two score and ten years ago," her school was established in her town, and so on. She shrugged her shoulders, obviously baffled, when she realized that everyone seemed very impressed. "I don't know how to write my own speech," she said. "The Gettysburg Address is the only speech I know, so I used it."

The final writing assignment one year was to write a fantasy about something that the child might like to do in the summer, with lots of descriptive detail. She could not and would not write about an imaginary experience. "I don't do that," she said. Unlike other Asperger children, who might be immobilized by this, Heidi decided that all she could do was to write about something that had already happened the previous summer. Details are right up her alley, so that part was easy. Her father read her essay and pointed out that it needed to be in the future tense. That was easy. She rewrote the essay in the future tense.

> This summer I plan to go to the beach. I will get in the car, and endure the loud shrieking of my sisters, my mom's MFM (Music for Minors), and my dad's lectures to make the family better. Soon we will have spotted water. In less than ten minutes, we will be on the street next to the sandy shore looking for a parking spot. As we walk through the litter-coated sidewalks, my sisters and I fight over who will get to play with my mom. When we get to the sand, we will take off our shoes so the sand doesn't get into them and hurt our feet. The sun-roasted sand burns our feet. Once our things are set up, we are ready to play.

I zoom into the water, with my clothes on, and totally soak myself. Then I run over to my mom, hug her, and have to have a short time out for getting her all wet. As soon as my punishment is over, I run back into the foamy white surf. It will turn me over and over, and I will not see above the greenish water until it decides to let me go. I will then go up to our camp and take a few pretzels in my hand and go back to the wet sandy part of the beach to look for shells. Soon it is close to dark and it is time for dinner. I like the sushi restaurant, so we go there. Since it is Sunday, and we have camp tomorrow, we have to go home early.

In the car, everybody is cranky. For one thing, the car smells like dead fish, for all of us haven't showered yet. Nobody wants to go home. Third, there is sand in all of the crevices and openings in our stinky bodies, and boy does it sting! It is in our ears, our eyes, our mouths, behind our ears, in our noses, in our hair, on our scalp, in our behinds, and in between our toes. By the time we get home, my sandy sisters are snoring loudly. Since it is so late, I don't have to brush my teeth.

There was nothing left for Heidi to do but title her essay. That was listed as a requirement of the assignment. It probably did not occur to her to have the title relate to the content (such as "A Day at the Beach"). She wanted to be finished with this assignment, but still needed a title. Then she thought of a title that satisfied her. She called this essay "Last Writing Project of the Year."

11

Afterword: What Lies Ahead

I have worked with AS children and their families, with other professionals, and with schools for many years. When we understand the child's thinking and meaning, and help him to understand himself, he generally manages what he can, one small, clearly articulated step at a time. I have seen this so often, I believe it will happen, and I expect it.

When adults and a child work together to make the present manageable, we may still be concerned about the years ahead. What lies ahead can seem much more formidable than what we have arranged for the present. Focusing on the future may overwhelm us. I have seen children who were so overwhelmed in grade school that they were unable to function much of the time, go on to manage and to do well later. It does not seem to matter how many times I have seen this. I still watch in amazement, almost in disbelief. These students often do well in high school and college, with struggles and with many successes. Children with Asperger minds can progress positively, if we pay attention to who they are, how they think, and how they communicate. We can make accommodations that support how they learn. This approach makes a difference.

Some AS children manage so well that they succeed in the mainstream without interventions, or with minimal support.

Aaron

Aaron struggled in elementary school, and at first resisted any intervention. He did not expect the "help" to be helpful. On the other hand, he was depressed, had angry outbursts, and difficulty understanding or tolerating other students and accepting direction from teachers. Once he understood more about his own mind, he became interested in figuring out how to be successful in school. Although he did not always agree with them, he did learn that school success depended on understanding the expectations of his teachers. His "Asperger thinking," though rigid at times, is part of who he is and how he sees the world. He does not really understand the concept of "flexible thinking." It can seem unclear and illogical to him. He has exact ideas of what is right and true. Yet Aaron developed a cognitive ability to articulate perspective, and learned the importance of understanding the perspective of the teacher or lesson (as wrong as he might think it is).

Aaron was very anxious about starting middle school, and tried to convince his parents to let him go to a smaller private school with only two classes for each grade. The public middle school had the same language therapist as his elementary school. She arranged for him to visit the school, to see the teachers, the classes, and how the students moved from class to class. With this visit in mind, he reluctantly began middle school the next fall, and found the environment familiar enough. Although Aaron continued to have an IEP, based on pragmatic language issues, the language therapist documented this only by observation. These issues could not be documented in pragmatic language testing, because Aaron could give the correct answers in a test situation. The language therapist served as a resource to the teachers and did not provide direct services, because Aaron was able to successfully complete middle school without direct services. Although Aaron was in a flexible and supportive school district, he wanted to attend a private high school. His parents were able to provide this for him, and supported his decision, because they lived in a large metropolitan area with two private schools that had a somewhat less traditional curriculum for bright, motivated students, a curriculum that seemed to be a good match for his interests and learning style.

John

John learned that he did not necessarily understand things in the same way that others do. He had many private and school supports and interventions in grade school. He also benefited from support through middle school, and continued to have the choice to have extra time for tests in high school and college. Other than this, and sensitive class selection, he did not have specific accommodations in his academic, public high school. While his science and math classes were on a higher track, he took English and literature classes that were adequate to meet college prep standards, but not as demanding or abstract as the higher tracks. By the time he entered college, he was able to manage his general education classes well enough. He and his family realized that once he completed his first two years, he would be able to focus on his area of interest, and also do much of his work in a department of interest with a more contained environment. After his freshman year, John "recuperated" by working the entire summer on a ship. This provided a very familiar environment and focused on an area of interest, with clear and predictable roles and expectations, and with others who had similar interests and abilities – heaven for him.

When children expect that something manageable will be worked out for the present, they begin to want to take on more. It helps them (and us) to know that taking on more can come with time and patience. If trying more is not successful, they and we can remember that smaller steps or greater support may be needed. That can be our focus. Many adolescent AS students, even those who are very bright and knowledgeable in many areas, cannot manage all of the mainstream education expectations by middle school or high school. They may be very successful, and continue to progress, with the accommodations and modifications that enable them to manage the present. Their understanding of themselves can enable them to be active participants in planning and utilizing the supports that they need.

Dan

Dan is the child who read excruciatingly slowly, because he did not understand the concept of a main idea without all the details, or how others could know it. He only understood concrete information and facts. Before he could read, Dan wanted to hear only factual books as bedtime stories, even when he was very young. Dan started having outside therapies and school accommodations and modifications in the early grades. Even with these, and with medication as well, he was anxious, isolated, depressed, unable to complete much work, and generally miserable in school. At home, he spent a good deal of time in his room, twirling a pencil to relax. He was so exhausted after school that it could take hours to complete a short assignment, even one that he understood and knew how to do. Working on something he did not fully understand could result in a complete meltdown by the evening.

Dan welcomed his individual therapy as a place he could be accepted for himself, a place to begin to know his own mind and try to make sense of others. This was without any expectation that he should change, although it could be a time to figure out what might make his life better. It was also an opportunity to plan changes in expectations that matched his needs, rather than changes he should make. By middle school, with teachers who were flexible and subjects he understood, Dan participated in special education classes for one or two periods during the day, but primarily in mainstream classes with modified assignments. In seventh grade, he was preparing to participate in an important family and religious event. During this time he was particularly overwhelmed. A special IEP team meeting was called, and the team agreed (although reluctantly) that he would be expected to work in school, but almost no homework would be expected for the last three months of the year. His test scores were good, because Dan could do well on most tests by relying on what he learned by listening and on his excellent memory and his understanding of logical concepts. Dan was an articulate participant in this and all future IEP meetings.

By eighth grade, Dan wanted to do more of his work, because he was concerned about his future. On the other hand, he did not think he could do this on his own. He was much more likely to feel angry, overwhelmed, and resistant to help from his parents than from a tutor. Dan's parents hired a tutor who came to his house after school for about two hours, four days a week. With his tutor, Dan completed most of the significantly modified workload. Dan asked for and explained his IEP modifications to his teachers when needed. He also requested that he be moved to a higher math class, and was more successful in a class that required understanding more than numerical accuracy. He still did less homework and needed extra time.

By the time he reached high school, Dan was able to do most of his math and science homework on his own. He only used his tutor once a week. He and the team agreed that he could be in a special education history class during his freshman year. Although he knew, or easily learned, most of the material, he also knew that there would be considerably fewer or shorter assignments in the special education history class. In that class, he did more than was required to complete assignments. Rather than a modified report (by class standards), he prepared an in-depth paper on a historical figure, one who he was quite sure had AS (because he recognized the man's Asperger mind and behavior). He consciously focused on his organization, as well as the content, and considered what others might be interested in hearing (not everything he knew) when he explained his report to the class.

For freshman English, Dan was in a mainstream, but not a college preparatory level, class. He began to understand the difficulty he had with writing assignments. In other classes, he could focus on the meaning of the question or problem. In English writing assignments, that did not work. He needed to focus on what the teacher (and sometimes what an author or character) might have in mind (other than factual information). This is not something Dan did, and he had never before understood that it was something that others did. He had not even known that this could be important to consider. His goal then became to communicate enough with his English teacher to determine whether he was on the right track, and then to correct his drafts as he wrote. This goal and process was written into his IEP, so he and his teacher understood clearly what he was doing and why.

Dan also had one period of "study skills" every day, a resource class in which students can get help with assignments. Dan used that time to do as much homework as possible, so he would have less to do in the evening. For the first time, Dan felt that he could handle school, and he was getting very good grades in all of his subjects. Although he did not have friends outside school (he needed and appreciated his "down time"), he was comfortable around and able to communicate with other students in his classes, as well as at lunch and other unstructured times.

For his sophomore year, Dan is taking a college preparatory, mainstream English class, and not taking history during the first semester. This English class is less demanding and less abstract than the honors level, but meets the University of California (UC) standards of admission. While he knows that he and his family will select a college that best meets his needs at the time, he wants to try to meet the UC admission standards. If he feels he can manage it, he plans to add mainstream history in the second semester (perhaps with some accommodations). In any case, he knows that he will do what he can, and take the time he needs to take. Dan and others who know him well are now confident of his ability to recognize when he is having difficulty and his ability to get help understanding and meeting his needs. Dan has a level of understanding of his own mind, and an attention to trying to understand and get along with others, that is well beyond that of many his age (or perhaps any age).

Children and adolescents like Dan show us that when we listen to AS students, when we accept them and treat them respectfully, we can learn together how they think and how they learn. When we create manageable learning environments together, these environments become the bedrock on which their future lies.

Instructional Assistance for an AS Child: Discovering the Child's Perspective

Julia M. Hara, a specialized instructional assistant (IA), was assigned to an AS child who needed direction, modifications, and accommodations. It can be difficult to remain open to listening to others, and to our own hearts and minds with reflection, in an environment in which few adults serve many children. For some students, the school environment is not a good fit. Then, learning from the child can be the basis of success. Julia recognized and articulated what many who work with children learn. If we start by understanding the child's mind and perspective, we learn from the child, and we receive as much from the process as we bring to it.

Julia wanted to know the child she was assisting. She was open to understanding the child's mind to develop meaningful interventions, and saw how this contributed to a collaborative relationship with the child. This inspired her to write about an experience she had with the child she is assisting.

A Day in the Life of a Specialized IA

It was a hot, late summer day. Nick had just started second grade. The school bell rang, and all the children knew that once again, recess was over. As Mrs Miller's students lined up neatly along the white line, Nick kept straying from that white line. Naturally, I asked him to move back to the line. There was no response. I prodded him gently on the back, pointing to *that white line*. Once again, my gesture went unnoticed. Before the situation got into a tug-of-war, I started looking in the direction that Nick was looking. It was then that I noticed his eyes were fixed on the ground with much intrigue. He swayed his body back and forth with great animation and delight, apparently entertaining himself, with a broad smile on his face. Now that got *me* intrigued! What was he staring at? What could be so funny and interesting? There was nothing on the ground except two fallen leaves, with the shadow of Nick's head right on the leaves. Suddenly, it dawned on me. There was a very important correlation between the shadow of his head and those two leaves ... his shadow had come alive with two eyes!!! As in a lightning revelation, I saw what I could do! I quickly moved the two leaves closer to the white line. Nick then lined up where he was supposed to be, with the rest of the class.

This is a true story of how I was enlightened to see beyond what was in front of my eyes and listen with more than my ears. I want to say that this is how specialized IA's can "entice" the cooperation of their students. We can, if we can only see with our minds and listen with our hearts. However, this is universally true with all human relationships.

I know there are literally tons of books and articles on the subject of special needs students. I do not profess to know or say anything new here. I just sincerely want to share this one of many, many, heart-warming and mind-opening experiences that Nick has brought me. If I can only look at him with a different light in my mind and listen to him with reflection in my heart, I can be mindful that he is, after all, different. Aren't we all?

Julia M. Hara, written in 2004. Reproduced with permission.

The child that Julia described, just one year later, was generally able to describe what he was thinking or doing. He still needed support, and sometimes needed individual help to "get" what the teacher expected when she gave assignments and instructions to the entire class, but he attended to and participated in teacher-led activities. He accepted assignments and wanted to complete them.

Julia Hara now participates in the orientation of instructional assistants in her district, describing this openness to knowing a child's perspective, and the importance of using what you learn to understand the child's mind, to solve problems, and to support the child.

Educating Peers about an Asperger Child

Pam Ehrlich is the parent of an Asperger child who co-wrote a sample reference binder, published in Jacobsen 2003. Below is a generic version of a classroom discussion she has led in her son's classrooms. This discussion was a very positive experience for her son (who was present) as well as for the other children and teacher.

Asperger talk

Mrs T (teacher's name) asked me to come and talk with you today. I am here to talk about C (child's name) and some of the ways that people can be different. C has something called Asperger Syndrome. Asperger Syndrome is not a bad thing to have. It is not a disease. It is a way to describe certain people. Saying someone has Asperger Syndrome says that they are great at knowing a lot of detailed facts, but not as good at understanding people. People with Asperger Syndrome think differently than other people. Thinking in this different way is a great thing, but makes it hard to understand people and for people to understand you.

There have been many famous people who did amazing things because they thought differently than other people. [Check "Asperger Syndrome and famous people" on the Internet to pick people whom the children in your child's class are likely to know and to be interested in.] One of the US Presidents, *Thomas Jefferson*, had trouble understanding people and many people thought he was strange because of how he acted and his detailed interests. *Albert Einstein*, a well-known physicist, was very smart, but had a lot of trouble getting along with people. *Thomas Edison* invented the light bulb, but when he was your age he was taught at home by his Mom because he couldn't sit still and he wanted to study his own interests. Raise your hand if you know anything about *Pokémon*. Did you know the creator of the amazing detailed world of Pokémon (Shatoshi Tijjaru) is great at knowing facts, but has trouble understanding people too? Many people believe that *Bill Gates*, the founder of Microsoft, is a lot like these other famous people. These people were great at thinking, but not as good at understanding people. These people did great things for the world, but they acted very differently than other people. When people think differently, it helps if their friends understand them. When their friends understand them better, their lives can be happier.

Tell me some of the things you have noticed about C

[Prepare differences to raise if they don't come up.]

C walks around the room (yard) – C notices details that many people don't notice, and that can make him tired faster. If he takes a break by walking, thinking, and even talking out loud, then he can sit and do a better job. It can be overwhelming to notice so many things every day.

Chews gummy things or his hands – This makes it easier for him to concentrate in a busy classroom or get rid of stress. Mrs P [principal's name] has given C special permission to chew gum when he needs to.

Leaves room with A [aide's name] – Sometimes he needs a break from all the noise and things going on in the classroom. He may cover his ears if there is a loud noise. He has very good hearing and notices things that other people might not.

Looks like he is not paying attention – It is easier to concentrate on people's words when he isn't watching their faces. C may put his head in his hands, sit in the library, lie on his chair, or walk back and forth.

Doesn't look when talking – It is hard for him to learn when looking at someone, too distracting from thinking.

Handwriting isn't neat – He likes to write and his thoughts come faster than he can write them down neatly.

Asperger Syndrome makes some things easier for C

[Prepare positives to raise if they don't come up.]

Special interests – When C is very interested in something, like Bionicles, US Presidents, spiders, insects, amphibians and reptiles, he learns every detail he can about his interest.

Reading books – C reads well and he reads everything he can about his special interests.

Spelling and facts – C is very good at learning and remembering how to spell words, and lots of facts. If I have trouble spelling a word, I ask C. If I can't remember something about one of the US presidents, I ask C. If he watches a TV show about insects, he will always remember the detailed facts he has heard. I am lucky if I remember some of the information for a week. He can often identify a spider by remembering the page from one of his identification guides.

Let's talk more about what Asperger Syndrome is

The best way for me to help you understand what Asperger Syndrome is, is to talk about the five senses.

1. Raise your hand to tell me the five senses: sight, hearing, touch, taste, smell.

2. Now, raise your hand if anyone taught you to see. No, you didn't have to learn it, you just knew it on your own, automatically. Everyone doesn't see or hear the same. Some people use hearing aids in order to hear well. What do people use so they can see better?

3. Did any one ever hear about another kind of sense? It is sometimes called the sixth sense (Gray 2002). It's our *social sense.*

Some people know automatically what other people feel or what they know. Some people can tell quickly if a game is over, if everyone wants to do something else, or if the rules have been changed. Other people don't know this automatically and they have to have help to figure it out. Over time, they can learn to figure it out themselves, but they need help from friends or teachers at the beginning so they can learn to do it on their own.

C is learning how to figure out what many other people already know – how to tell what other people feel and know. He is learning how to watch other people so that he can know when a game is ending and when a group wants to change the rules. His friends know him and know that C is working on this, so they help him. Mrs A [aide] is there to help C learn how to use his sixth sense better. Sometimes she will point things out to him so that he will know what to look for – kind of like a coach for a soccer team. She can help him see what are the important details. This helps him so he will know what to look for next time. Mrs A also helps other students because C doesn't need her help all of the time.

Raise your hand if you have ever had a goal to learn how to do something new or better – like riding a bike, shooting a basketball, drawing a better picture, playing piano, learning a new swimming stroke.

Now, raise your hand if you had help from a friend, a teacher, or a grown-up so that you could do things better.

Everyone has things that they want to work on, and most of those things need help from someone else. C is like everyone else. He has things that he wants to do better at and he can learn them faster with the help of friends and teachers.

What are the ways you can help your friends play with you and understand you? [Be prepared with a list to suggest, if they don't come up.]

1. Follow [school's name] rules – no pushing or pulling at school.

2. Treat others the way you want to be treated. (Don't play rough if you don't want to be treated rough.)

3. If you have a problem with someone, stop what you are doing, then talk it through. (If you are having trouble helping C understand something, Mrs A is great at helping both people.)

4. Don't know what to do at recess or lunch? (Suggest places to play.)

5. Talk about the things that interest you. Everyone can find a topic that they can talk about. (C reads the Bionicles and Star Wars websites, along with books about spiders, insects and reptiles.)

I know a lot of kids like C, smart kids who act differently than people expect them to. I know even more grown-ups like C and they are kind, talented people who do amazing things when they are at work and at home.

One of the things you may know is that C is a kind, fair and honest friend. C is like everyone else, he likes to have friends and to be a good friend. C likes to help other people. C likes some time by himself, and he also likes to be included like everyone else. Everyone likes to have friends to play and talk with.

Have you noticed that C may act differently, but in other ways he is like everyone else? C is a kind friend, who likes to help. Each of us is different in one way or another, but all of us need help from friends and teachers.

C and I hope this helps you understand him better. Mrs T and Mrs A, do you think I have covered everything? Are there any questions? [One catch phrase to emphasize, whenever it fits with what comes up, is "Great at knowing facts, but not as good at understanding people."]

Pam Ehrlich, C's mother, gave a version of this talk every year since kindergarten. One year, at the end of the talk, a teacher added, "This week we have been talking about my goal for all of you this year. My goal is that by the end of the year, you will understand what kind of learner you are, and what strategies work for you to help you do your best work. It may be that you make a list of the steps you need to do in an assignment. It may be that a diagram helps you understand how things work. All of us can benefit by knowing how we think and what strategies work well for us." This supported that all the students develop awareness of themselves, as well as acceptance of differences in others.

An Observation at a Specialized School for Asperger Students

In 2002 I visited the Orion Academy in Moraga, California, a small private secondary school that specializes in providing a positive academic experience for students with Asperger Syndrome. This observation convinced me that it was definitely possible to provide a high level (college prep) curriculum in an "Asperger-friendly" way. In the classes I observed, all students were required to type notes on their laptop computers. The manner in which this was done made it possible for the students who were in the class. This is the kind of program that could be effective (in public as well as private schools) for AS students who are capable of learning in the right environment, but are having a great deal of difficulty in the mainstream. Some AS students might have difficulty typing notes all of the time, and may handle a high-level curriculum with a note taker or by being provided with teacher notes (especially if the students are expected to pay attention to anything else while writing).

Orion Academy observation, October 20 2002

The students exhibited a range of Asperger and NLD (Nonverbal Learning Disorder) behaviors and communication styles. The class size was small (about ten students), and each student used a laptop computer. They were all able to participate and learn in the school environment. They seemed comfortable being around each other, and many spent the recess crowded on a couch, standing near it, or walking.

Sophomore literature

In this class the desks were arranged in a circular fashion. The teacher could see each student, and the students could see each other. The content of the literature lesson was a passage from Thoreau's *Walden*. The experience of the lesson was like that of a meaningful, interactive language and cognition lesson. The teacher read a short passage three different times during the lesson, first very slowly and each subsequent time a little faster. He addressed what Thoreau said, identifying it as Thoreau's opinion. He separately addressed the students' thoughts, reactions, or other responses to Thoreau's perspective, and the students' own opinions and preferences. This focus on recognizing the author's perspective, and their own, underlines the awareness and perspective that needs to be articulated to be recognized (in an overt, cognitive way) by these students (but is so often expected or assumed, without being articulated).

The students were to write a sentence about Thoreau's meaning in one column on their laptop computers, and a sentence about their opinion in the second column. Each student read what he had written on his computer, and the teacher articulated what related to Thoreau's opinions and what was an example of the student's thoughts, always clarifying each. He responded to the students' comments that were relevant, taking the opportunity to restate their comments using the vocabulary of literature, which they could probably define, but might not have recognized. He responded to other comments that they made that were tangential (from our perspective, but important to the student) by briefly clarifying or addressing the student's need or concern and then redirecting to the assignment.

The teacher explained that the homework assignment was to read 15 pages without trying to understand them, to read the words whether or not they made any sense to the student (in other words, they could go on, not get stuck, when it did not make sense, because "trying to understand" was not part of this particular assignment). Then the student needed to find one sentence that he or she understood (just one sentence), and write what the student thought Thoreau meant and, separately, the student's own response or thoughts about it. Exactly what they did in class.

Biology

The biology lesson was a lecture and discussion about cells. In discussion, students shared what they knew and the teacher repeated what was important to the subject, and why. The teacher answered the most concrete questions in a direct fashion, taking them at face value (which was clearly how they were meant). For example, the teacher said that all living things were made of cells. One student asked if that meant only living things. The teacher said, matter-of-factly, that formerly living things (such as a stick that was once part of a tree) were also made of cells.

The students copied the clear, organized notes that the teacher had written on the board. She articulated the relevance of the organization of the material, even noting the details that were not relevant to the way it was written on the board. For example, she explained that she had some information in two columns to fit it on the board. This particular information could be written in one list on the computer or in two columns, a matter of preference (in this case) rather than meaning or importance. They finished discussing some of the material, the teacher clarified that the students understood, and she then waited while they were copying their notes. During this time, she walked behind each row and looked at the computers. She then returned to the front of the class, stating that she would erase this material. She told them that she had walked around and looked at their screens, and it looked as if they were all just about finished, but she wanted to know if anyone still needed time. There couldn't have been any question in a student's mind about what the teacher was thinking, why she was thinking it, what she was doing, what was expected, and why. Watching her reminded me of what a boy once said to me. We were playing Mastermind, something we are both pretty good at, although each of us uses a somewhat different strategy. "I know how your mind figures this out," he said, "because you talk out loud while you're thinking." This is exactly what the teacher was doing as she talked to the class. They knew her thoughts, because she said them out loud, no matter how "obvious" they might seem to many people.

Impressions

Someone who is not aware of the needs of an AS student might think that not a whole lot happens in these classes. If the important, right, things (match for the student's needs and strengths) are happening, that is plenty. In the two classes I observed, the methods of instruction and expectations, as well as the relationship of the teacher with the student, were suited to the needs of these students. This clearly requires teachers who are patient and who are interested in and responsive to the needs and abilities of the students.

After visiting this school, I had the nagging feeling that there was something else that I was missing, something that I could not quite articulate to myself. It came to me several days later. I observed a number of behaviors and I heard many of the very concrete or somewhat unrelated comments and questions that are perfectly sensible from the perspective of these students (and part and parcel of the gifts they sometimes have). The difference was that when these things happened, no adult or child made a sarcastic comment or laughed. No one rolled his eyes or imitated another person. This may be why most students "hung out" near others; they were reasonably comfortable with their peers.

References

American Psychiatric Association (1994) *Diagnostic and Statistical Manual of Mental Disorders,* 4th edn. Washington, DC: American Psychiatric Association.

Attwood, T. (1998) *Asperger's Syndrome: A Guide for Parents and Professionals.* London: Jessica Kingsley Publishers.

Baron-Cohen, S., Leslie, A.M. and Frith, U. (1985) 'Does the autistic child have a "theory of mind"?' *Cognition 21,* 37–46.

Baron-Cohen, S., Ring, H.A., Wheelwrights *et al.* (1999) 'Social intelligience in the normal and autistic brain: An fMRI study? *European Journal of Neuroscience II, 6,* 1891–8.

Bellugi, U. (2001) (Stimuli and drawings for global and local processing) © Dr Ursula Bellugi, The Salk Institute for Biological Studies, La Jolla, CA 92037.

Bihrle, A.M., Bellugi, U., Delis, D. and Marks, S. (1989) 'Seeing either the forest or the trees: Dissociation in visuospatial processing.' *Brain and Cognition 11,* 37–49.

Buron, K.D. and Curtis, M. (2004) *The Incredible 5-Point Scale: Assisting Students with Autism Spectrum Disorders in Understanding Social Interactions and Controlling their Emotional Responses.* Shawnee Mission, KA: Autism Asperger Publishing Co.

Cumine, V., Leach, J. and Stevenson, G. (1998) *Asperger Syndrome: A Practical Guide for Teachers.* London: David Fulton Publishers.

Frith, U. (1989) *Autism: Explaining the Enigma.* Oxford: Blackwell.

Gray, C. (2000) 'The social story kit.' In C. Gray (ed) *The Original Social Story Book.* Arlington, TX: Future Horizons and *The New Social Story Book: Illustrated Edition.* Arlington, TX: Future Horizons.

Gray, C. (2002) *The Sixth Sense II.* Arlington, TX: Future Horizons.

Happé, F. (October 21, 1997) 'Autism: Understanding the mind, fitting together the pieces.' London: Francesca Happé and Mindship International. (www.mindship.org/happe.htm)

Jacobsen, P. (2003) *Asperger Syndrome and Psychotherapy: Understanding Asperger Perspectives.* London: Jessica Kingsley Publishers.

Jacobsen, Paula (2004) 'A brief overview of the principles of psychotherapy with Asperger Syndrome.' *In Clinical Child Psychology and Psychiatry 9,* 4, 556–78.

King, D.H. (1986) *Keyboarding Skills.* Cambridge, MA: Educators Publishing Service, Inc. (800–225–5750)

Klin, A., Jones, W., Schultz, R. and Volkmar, F. (2003) 'The enactive mind, or from actions to cognition: lessons from autism.' *Phil. Trans. Royal Society,* 358: 345–60.

Lotspeich, L. (2001) 'Recognizing and understanding Asperger's Syndrome in your clinical practice.' Presentation at the Cleo Eulau Center Continuing Education Symposium, 3 November.

Mitchell, P. (1997) *Introduction to Theory of Mind: Children, Autism, and Apes.* London: Hodder Arnold.

Moore, S.T. (2002) *Asperger Syndrome and the Elementary School Experience: Practical Solutions for Academic and Social Difficulties.* Shawnee Mission, KA: Autism Asperger Publishing Co.

Parish, P. (1991) *Amelia Bedelia.* USA: Harper Collins Publishers.

Piggot, J. (2004) 'Emotional attribution in high-functioning individuals with Autism Spectrum Disorder: A functional imaging study.' *Journal of the American Academy of Child and Adolescent Psychiatry 43*, 4, 473–80.

Schultz, R.T., Gauthier, I., Klin, A., *et al.* (2000) 'Abnormal ventral temporal cortical activity during face discrimination among individuals with autism and Asperger Syndrome.' *Archives of General Psychiatry 57*, 4, 331–40.

Silberman, S. (2001) 'The geek disease.' *Wired*, 174–83 (www.wired.com)

Wheelwright, S. and Baron-Cohen, S. (2001) 'The link between autism and skills such as engineering, maths, physics and computing.' *Autism 5*, 2, 223–7.

Williams, J.H.G., Whiten, A., Suddendorf, T. and Perrett, D. (2004) 'Imitation, mirror neurons, and autism.' In *Neuroscience and Biobehavioral Reviews 25*, 4, 287–95.

Winnicott, D.W. (1965) *The Maturational Process and the Facilitating Environment.* New York: International Universities Press.

Winnicott, D.W. (1992) *The Child, the Family, and the Outside World.* London: Perseus.

Index

Note: page numbers in *italics*
refer to diagrams